New & Selected Poems

of

John Weier

LYRIK POETRY SERIES 2

Series Editor: Nathan Dueck

Do not doubt the odd
diphthonic measure of these words
now between absurdity and pleasure
Between the forecast and the weather

New & Selected Poems

of

John Weier

Edited and with an introduction
by Nathan Dueck

CMU PRESS
WINNIPEG, MANITOBA
2025

CMU PRESS

CMU Press
Canadian Mennonite University
500 Shaftesbury Blvd.
Winnipeg MB R3P2N2
www.cmupress.ca

CMU Press is learning and striving to create an inclusive and welcoming space for people of many identities and communities. We work on land which is the ancestral home of the Anishinaabe, Cree, Dakota, and Métis peoples. We are grateful for their stewardship of this place.

The publication of this book has received financial support from the Gerhard Lohrenz Publication Fund, administered by Canadian Mennonite University.

Series Editor: Nathan Dueck
Copyeditor: Sue Sorensen
Editorial assistance: Phil Waldner, Javier Jiménez
Cover and interior design: Jonathan Dyck

Printed in Canada by Friesens Corporation, Altona, Manitoba.
ISBN 978-1-987986-16-7

Library and Archives Canada Cataloguing in Publication

Title: New & selected poems of John Weier / edited and with an introduction by Nathan Dueck.
Other titles: New and selected poems of John Weier
Names: Weier, John, 1949- author. | Dueck, Nathan, 1979- editor, writer of introduction
Description: Series statement: Lyrik poetry series ; 2 | Includes bibliographical references and index.
Identifiers: Canadiana 20240479068 | ISBN 9781987986167 (softcover)
Subjects: LCGFT: Poetry.
Classification: LCC PS8595.E418 N49 2025 | DDC C811/.54—dc23

---

always, for Jonathan and Anna

CONTENTS

New Poems
Refuge

Afterword

Introduction

Nathan Dueck

Religion is one topic society somehow determined isn't suitable for polite conversation. I'm not sure how that consensus came about—why do we assume that discussing faith will only lead to disagreement?—but I can't say that I agree. And, given what I know of John Weier from his poetry, I'm guessing he's with me (or, more appropriately, I'm with him). He has written at some length over his lifetime about religion, both in terms of personal beliefs and institutional doctrines, and often in challenging and occasionally confrontational ways. But, if you'll allow me to talk publicly about faith, I'll follow Weier's lead and confess that I, too, question mine all the time. While we're at it, if you'll permit me to flout manners for a few pages, why not address political opinions and sexual confusion as Weier would? And, hey, what's keeping us from chatting about financial concerns, too? (And here you thought Weier mostly wrote about travel and birds and travelling to see birds.) It would seem to me that delving into those matters is permissible so long as I'm willing to take in vulnerability and make myself vulnerable in turn. A combination of candour and culpability is what makes Weier's poetry compelling. Although the speakers therein have strong convictions, and they can be contrarian on occasion, they never seem to be wholly committed to their own arguments. They question others as well as themselves. Weier articulates this state of uncertainty with sensitivity, and by so doing, he invites genuine reaction.

WEIER'S AESTHETIC

Before I get carried away, let's consider some essential aspects of Weier's aesthetic. An ideal reader would accept the verbal irony in these poems as invitational provocations. By contrast, a less-than-ideal reader would reject it as incitement, something akin to advocating for an adversary. The poem that concludes the collection *Violinmaker's Lament*, "Violins and poetry 1995," demonstrates this contrasting dynamic. The first line, "I am a poor man," prompts the reader to ascertain if this statement is sincere. If so, the poem would appear to be a plea for sympathy; if not, it could seem a disingenuous ploy. Of course, it could be both or neither, a claim that can only be pondered and never definitively proven. Having established that, we'll proceed by agreeing upon the premise that in this poem Weier presents poverty as a metaphor.

Anaphora, the repetition of key words at the beginning of lines, is the primary structural technique of "Violins and poetry 1995" as most lines start with I am, I have, or I had. In the tradition of lyric poetry, Weier himself is undoubtedly the subject of this poem. Still, such self-assertion establishes the presence of the speaker while simultaneously questioning the very notion of epistemological subjectivity. Which is to say, Weier asserts himself through the speaker of this poem, except he knows that we know he has previously written other poems featuring other speakers, and he will write more poems featuring even more speakers later, so the concept of his self is changeable. The second stanza repeats that "I have holes in my pockets," suggesting that the speaker may be impoverished for real. This economic concern is urgent as he acknowledges "I need to pay the mortgage and the rent." Presumably, the speaker isn't living at home, and the costs of living are piling up. In the third stanza, though, he reasserts the opening line of the poem before using a simile that complicates any straightforward interpretation. Then the speaker asserts "I am poor as a poet" who has become receptive to "the thought of old places / dead friends." Thing is, this sort of "poverty" isn't even a little redemptive because, as the speaker puns, "I find nothing holy there." Paradoxically, the fourth stanza ends with "I have empty pockets," but the speaker proposes "I am a rich man" because "I have my honour   my honesty / I love my family / love my friends." The poem is only half-way through, and the poverty conceit has already moved from having no money to having nobody, and, finally, to having found some company to commiserate with.

With the remainder of the poem, the speaker settles on that topic of community as a remedy for impoverishment. The sixth stanza aligns his two occupations, luthier and poet:

I'm a poet praying in my prison
a craftsman tangled in his trade
I have subtracted my worth from my debt
zero is a human number

After that accounting, which indicates how the quality of being human isn't reducible to contribution to GDP, the speaker expresses why he writes poems. The meaning is that writing counts for more than money: it illuminates humanity. In the penultimate stanza, the speaker wishes that contact with "the song of that blue bird" and "the scarlet of the tanager" could "fill the hole of my missing children." Those lines appear to explain why the speaker's repeats, "I have holes in my pockets / I am a poor man." It would appear his occupation, along with other, less noble preoccupations, has come between the speaker and his offspring. The speaker redefines himself in the last stanza, stating "I am a beggar / I have nothing left to lose." The speaker wants an audience, and since this declaration appears in a poem, he must be hoping the reader will serve that function. "[T]here were beggars before the revolution," the speaker notes, and "there are beggars after the revolution / there are beggars here in Canada." Presumably, the revolution will take place within the space of a poem, placing the speaker beside his audience, even though they're seldom on the same page.

WEIER'S AFFECT

Weier often writes poems that strike a specific tone, one where speakers disguise their sincerity as insincerity. This allows them to assume various positions, some strongly held, others less so, as a ruse to arouse thought. To better understand how the reader might encounter such verbal irony, I'll turn to Sianne Ngai's description of tone as "unfelt but perceived feeling" (28). In *Ugly Feelings*, Ngai argues that "tone is never entirely reducible to a reader's emotional response to a text or reducible to the text's internal representations of feeling" (30). The trouble with interpretation is that tone isn't necessarily an indicator of reliability. Authorial intention isn't particularly trustworthy either. "We project the feeling that the object [text] inspires," Ngai suggests, "to create a *distance* between ourselves and that feeling" (85). That distance opens a space for "aesthetic engagement," says Ngai, whereby the readers determine for themselves what they are feeling and then determine how to let their feelings inform their interpretation. Returning to "Violins and poetry 1995," it seems to me that Weier's speaker is in the mood for a good argument. However, an author's emotional state is no more reliable than the reaction of the irritated, agitated, or annoyed reader. So, I'll just say the poem's speaker could be either striving to persuade or spoiling for a fight—regardless, he's starving for spirited discussion.

Reading poetry by Weier frequently means considering one's reaction to provocation. Ngai presents a useful analogy of the dial tone to illustrate how a literary text might inspire a particular response (51). The question, then, is how to answer the call. Ngai describes that while reading *The Confidence Man* it appears as though Melville

constructed [the narrative] for the purpose of giving the reader the unpleasant feeling of ironies constantly missed or passing over her head —that is, the meta-ironic feeling of an irony intended for and available to everyone but oneself. (51)

Now, nowhere in his poetry is Weier nearly as facetious as Melville in that novel, but the speaker of "Violins and poetry 1995" is a more than a little ironic, and possibly even sarcastic. So, I must determine if the call is for me at all; I might misunderstand. And, since that's the domain of affect theory, I'll turn to Sara Ahmed for guidance. In *The Cultural Politics of Emotion*, Ahmed theorizes that affect articulates a bodily response to a stimulus, one that precedes thought, but that doesn't mean we should consider it irrational or "the unthought" (170). To do so, she contends, would reify the hierarchical-cum-patriarchal relationship between thought and emotion.

Instead, we must consider how we come to understand how emotion is a construction of the self and others. Although one might precede the other (a pounding heart precedes an awkward phone conversation), they operate closely and in relation to each other (an awkward phone conversation prolongs the pounding heart). Both are signs of knowledge that

> cannot be separated from the bodily world of feeling and sensation; knowledge is bound up with what makes us sweat, shudder, tremble, all those feelings that are crucially felt on the bodily surface, the skin surface where we touch and are touched by the world. (171)

Emotional resonance, subjective though it may be, is a stimulus for interpretation. Another, perhaps more objective, component would seem to require coming to terms with several semantic and semiotic possibilities. So, applying this analysis to "Violins and poetry 1995," I suspect it's necessary to feel provoked in order to engage its aesthetic.

To support my reading, I'll briefly turn to Lauren Berlant's *On the Inconvenience of Other People*. Berlant defines her use of "inconvenience" as "the affective sense of the familiar friction of being in relation," or, more specifically, "the force that makes one shift a little while processing the world" (2). In that way, inconvenience is one form of intensity that applies to reading literature just as easily as real life interactions. (In fact, Berlant addresses how inconvenience evolved when we all took safety precautions to prevent the spread of COVID-19. I'd add that reading literature produced a profound sense of friction while we were socially distancing. As much as I wanted to turn away from the world and read, say, the poems of Weier, the reading experience almost felt too intense.) To describe the push and pull function of inconvenience, Berlant summons Theodor Adorno's conception of the *shudder* one feels on "receiving the aesthetic object [which] registers the intimate effects of an abstract, yet affectively personal, transaction with the world" (18). In his short essay "Theories on the Origin of Art: Excursus," Adorno articulates how the shudder is "the reaction to the total spell that transcends the spell." This affective response encompasses more than the literary text. Even in the author's absence, a sense of "subjectivity stirs without yet being subjectivity," almost as though the reader is "being touched by the other" (311). This shudder results either from empathy for those depicted by the text, or, as people tend to say these days, from being "seen." This sort of engagement helps explain my conflicted response to "Violins and poetry 1995." I can hardly believe Weier talks that way about poverty; but, at the same time, I can hardly believe that I think the same way he does about poetry. So, yes, occasionally feeling my blood pressure rise while reading is a significant part of what I like to call The Weier Experience. It moves me to invest emotional and intellectual energies in the making of meaning—and maybe even in the making of community.

THE WEIER EXPERIENCE

To illustrate what I mean by that term, I'll survey some poems that encapsulate how Weier presents the reader with the opportunity for such an experience, both in form and theme. Weier relies on three formal elements to make it seem as though his poems feel conversational: he prefers plain over figurative language; he often relies on repetition and reiteration; and, he freely combines poetry and prose.

Take "Violinmaker / September 12" from *Violinmaker's Lament*. The poem's speaker is a diarist considering poverty while recalling a "lazy" morning at work. While the speaker enjoys a mug of morning coffee and "a cigarette / from the pack Sara keeps in the freezer," unexpected company arrives. All the "visitor / beggar" asks for is "a dollar / two dollars   twenty-five cents," so the speaker hands it over, and while doing so considers "the line between us   him and me." One line later, the speaker reconsiders whether that delineation represents "difference [or] similarity." In that moment of introspection, which is in keeping with a diary entry, the content of the piece aligns with its form. Those lines about lines contain a space that serves as both a comma and a caesura: the comma offers a pause without punctuation; the caesura offers the reader a space to meditate upon the relationship between strangers. "Violinmaker / September 12" ends with a reflection on the "rules of the game" that were imparted through "those lessons of youth" whereby we learn to ignore "hunger   revolution   civil war." The typographical space between those nouns paradoxically divides and unites at the same time. The speaker ends by stating those abstractions are "always packaged / together   violin / and bow / and string." That conclusion is the only metaphor in the poem, with the bow standing in for the line that is apart from the violin, but a part of its performance.

The speaker of "Violinmaker / September 12" demonstrates an important theme in Weier's poetry by commenting wryly on how changeable the self can be. Such self-consciousness encourages the reader to play along. By that I mean the poem urges an emotional response, even though the reader knows the speaker can't possibly hear. This experience is a ploy that Weier develops over his career as his poems become increasingly interested in breaking down and rebuilding how the poetic speaker functions. The culmination of this interest is the concept that the existence of the speaking subject is contingent on being read.

it's time

i leave
the sunlit prairie

With the chapbook *After the Revolution* (1986), Weier begins an exploration of family by focusing first on a father figure. A prose poem that appears early in the collection relates the speaker's memories helping "my dad" plant lines of stone fruit trees on their seven-acre farm, "cherry   peach   plum." That description aligns with Weier's recollections of moving from the prairies to a farm in the Niagara Fruit Belt in the 1950s ("Six Mennonite Stories" 203). Elsewhere, in the lyric poem "father," Weier characterizes the titular man of the house by what he does for a living. Before he took to cultivating trees, "my father" laboured in a fire "at his anvil" to "shape / the iron." And the speaker recalls with admiration how his father "doesn't fear / the fire." Switching to the third person for the poem "Black and White," Weier narrates the memory of "the boy" who simply wished "his father / would tell him" that his crayon colouring "was / pretty." The fully grown first-person speaker of "just like in the pictures" tests his mettle by working high-paying jobs—"six figure / salary   benefits falling / from the pockets of a hundred / three-piece suits"—while pursuing a woman—"you know / the one   wearing the perfume / that makes me dash off." A central conceit of *After the Revolution* is how the poetic speaker emerges from the shadow cast by a paternal influence. The good life can only follow a revolution, which might either occur when the son feels as masculine as the father or once the proletariat throws off their chains.

These revolutionary ideas culminate in the lyric poem "the clearing," when the speaker who goes by the lowercase "i" declares "it's time // i leave / the sunlit prairie." Before departing, he walks through "bounded / fields of grain   fenced / pastures   to touch / the forest." Entering the clearing of the title, he lies down, "skin / white against / the ground," and senses his "body / melting / into timeless / motion." Facedown on the tall grass, this body absorbs that feeling of eternity like "a new moon" overhead. In the eponymous poem "After the Revolution," the speaker, now an adult, describes how a particular woman "[h]e hasn't seen, or even thought of … for at least ten years" suddenly came to mind. He remembers the day when "[s]he'd come down to his basement shop to have her violin repaired" and they eventually developed a relationship. "She slept, ate, and breathed the revolution," and she had once "vaulted out of bed" to assure "John" that the "good life" is nigh at hand. She pledged to send him "to Italy" one day to "study with the world's best violin experts." Needless to say, that promise never came true, so he had to find "craftsmen in England and Hungary" to learn from. Having mastered a job and a developed a mature relationship, the son surpasses his father. Only, whereas the father laboured in midday heat, the son remarks that the wind at midnight blows cold.

⁓⁓⁓⁓⁓⁓

> a teacher of mine thinks that loneliness can best be
> described in terms of an empty chair. it's a good idea,
> but somehow tonight i can't find a chair large or
> strong enough

In his first full-length collection *Ride the Blue Roan* (1988), Weier continues the autobiographical exploration he initiated in *After the Revolution*, only this time he looks at maternal influence. In the hybrid poem "childhood and russia," the first-person speaker considers the consequences of revolution in "his mother's Russia." The complication, though, is that "she never spoke of it." After losing her mother "when she was two" and her "father when she was four," the mother was raised by family "during the revolution." The speaker traces his maternal family's immigration to Canada by ship in 1926, describing how "the aunt's children were buried at sea" but "his mother, the / stepchild, survived." After she fled certain death under Soviet rule, his mother lost "her first child" at the age of two, so she wondered if "things would be better in heaven" because she's endured "death / so much death" before arriving in the New World. Meanwhile, in the second part of the poem, the speaker's father, "at seventy-six" recollects "the village in russia" with longing for its annual celebration "after the threshing / is done on his father's farm." Whereas the mother ponders a deliverance to paradise, the father yearns to relive "the best / years of his life" back in the garden. The poem ends by commenting on that paradox: "what a / beautiful / tragedy."

Weier's speaker in the lyric poem "inheritance" strives for a space between those contradictory views. This occurs while he's "out driving" with his "son and daughter" across "the misericordia bridge." The birds perched overhead remind the speaker of "swallows [that] lived in / grandfather's barn" where "my father, still a boy, waited for / them in spring." The speaker ponders that beautiful tragedy when considering that he similarly awaited "nesting swallows to enter" the barn on the Niagara farm where he was raised. His children, though, grew up urban, so they don't recognize swallows or catch onto their "chattering song." The common ornithological know-how that was passed down over two generations is lost on them. It's difficult to cross the bridge from the past into a state of mercy.

The poem "woman talk" develops another subject that Weier often returns to in his work, troubled relationships with women. The speaker of this lyric relates three encounters that end without resolution. In the first, "a man sits at a table in the cafeteria" and makes intense eye contact with a woman walking by who's "carrying coffee." He strikes up a conversation until "suddenly   she looks at her watch" and exits the scene. Although this first liaison is brief, the second begins with a smile of intention and later ends in physical intimacy: "man's tongue / woman's body   together they speak forgotten / languages." The third encounter ends in unsettling silence, as the woman who "needed some space" refuses to return the speaker's calls. It's tempting to interpret the title "woman talk" as ironic because the three women featured in the poem don't say very much. The first woman chats briefly, the second woman speaks with gestures, and the third woman no longer communicates. Then again, apart from the proof of the poem itself, the reader can't tell whether the speaker himself is any kind of communicator. And, as the lyric poem "in terms of an empty chair" attests, Weier's speakers know more than a little about loneliness. After admitting "tonight, i'm lonely," the speaker recalls "a teacher of mine" who explained loneliness "in terms of an empty chair." In this moment, however, he "can't find a chair large or / strong enough." This metaphor exemplifies how Weier's poetry becomes especially self-conscious when coming to terms with loneliness.

Self-consciousness becomes spiritual in "buddha and the boat." This prose poem features the speaker reflecting on an experience of being on the shore and watching a man standing alone on a boat. He wonders if "the man is peter," referencing a miraculous passage from the gospels. The speaker questions "if / i'll hear a voice and the water will suddenly be still." But no such calming word is heard. Instead, "he says we're sailing. the storm / is too loud, he hasn't heard clearly." After the speaker clarifies, he hears "yes. he must have / taken me out here for a reason. There's something he / wishes to show me"; only the nature of that thing isn't clear. Apparently pondering that point is the point. It is a meditative poem without a specific *koan*. Weier will develop that turn away from Christian references and toward Buddhist principles in books that follow.

Ride the Blue Roan ends with two sections of epistolary poetry. These excerpts offer fragmented glimpses into Weier's creative process. The entry dated "12/10/86," for example, presents an anecdote suitable for a poem about the speaker's father: "in russia when father was young, he was told to / prepare for the trip to canada . . . by sea," so he "spen[t] as / much time swinging as possible" as a ploy to fend off seasickness. Such preparation, possibly verging on obsession, appears as a prominent theme in these confessional poems. Elsewhere, the speaker mentions how he fine-tunes instruments in his mind, even when his hands are still. Such a sentiment lends itself to an allegorical interpretation of how finds himself mentally composing poems while completing quotidian tasks. Such a reading even extends to his account of a romantic relationship where he cannot explain to a lover why he is compelled to behave the way he does.

Before continuing, I need to comment on the Mennoniteness of this discussion. I've refrained from referring to Weier by his ethnic heritage in respect of his wishes — or at least those he expressed in 1989. In a short, provocative article published in *Mennonite Mirror*, "Where Am I Now? Or Why I Am Not a Mennonite," Weier offers a list of ten theses that I want to subtitle "Declaration on the Uselessness of Cultural Indulgence" because he appears to renounce his Mennonite identity—e.g., church membership—while disclosing that he still indulges in identifiable Mennonite behaviours—e.g., eating cottage cheese perogies in heavy cream sauce mixed with fried sausage drippings. After admitting "I just don't believe what Mennonites are supposed to believe," Weier relates an anecdote that when he was a child at home, "I told my mother that I thought Hindus would probably go to heaven just like the rest of us." This thesis, the sixth, ends with the assertion, "I still don't think Mennonites have a better grip on God's coattails than Hindus or Buddhists or some native shaman. I just don't believe it." Weier then considers whether "[l]anguage has something to do with it." He's not talking about Plautdietsch (or, Low German) *per se*, which he assures the reader he speaks fluently. Instead, he asserts that "[t]he language of belief" doesn't speak to him because "the words I hear from the pulpit" can't address "why marriages fail" or come to terms with "the paintings I see at the gallery, the books I read, or write" (Weier, "Where am I Now" 26). In a public lecture delivered twenty-six years later, Weier elaborates that his early "church experience" involved three elements: "Hard words. Black and white thinking. Not much grace" ("Six Mennonite Stories" 207). The tenth and final thesis provides a meaningful basis for considering Weier's career: "The longer I live," he reveals, "the more I read and write and see, the more I let myself be who I am, the greater the gap between Mennonites and me" ("Where I am now" 26). He directs his last words to the Mennonite audience: "Maybe there can be no real bridge. But I can at least write to you. And someday we might get together, talk." Weier's biographical explorations in literary form are a type of idiosyncratic conversation with history.

I'll tell you my secrets little book
but listen
never let me write
anything
that's not my own

The next book of poetry in Weier's body of work is an engaging outlier. In his self-published chapbook *Twelve Poems for Emily Carr* (1994), Weier assumes the persona of the Canadian modernist artist of the title. The collection is a sequence of imaginary entries that appear to be excerpted from Carr's journals between 1930–1940. In Weier's telling, Carr records "happenings" by confiding in this "little book" while requesting that it "never let me write / anything / that's not my own" ("Journal January 23, 1930"). Of course, the irony of this opening poem is that here we have the poet ventriloquizing a historical figure who is very much not his "own." In the poem "September 9, 1933," "Carr" repeats the refrain "how / do you / paint," starting with "sky   the / tall tree pushing the slope in the corner," moving to "the world / from Beacon Hill," down into "sea sky no / horizon the pink grass leaning," around "the / house and its rooms," and finally to "sound   wind." The answers are not forthcoming, so the poem ends where it started: "how / do you / paint / that." Then again, the words flow when describing growth, wisdom, and rhythm. On "August 16, 1933," "Carr" returns to that question, "painted all / week but caught nothing so then what's the use how do you / paint a mountain a landscape" before opening it up to ask "how / do you look see how do you know / if I could just know that my painting moved / someone or joy gave them joy." The tone of that reflection, of the loneliness of the artist living outside of a community, contrasts with the first line of "October 3, 1939," where "Carr" asks "how do you paint / the war the howling / war." That question is pressing when we note that the Second World War began only one month earlier. The second part of "October 3, 1939" poses the converse question "how do you / paint / the peace of this / cabin." In a way, "Carr" contrasts the horrors unfolding in war-torn Europe with the breath-taking serenity of Vancouver Island. And it is that serenity that provides her with the space to represent emotions across the canvas of a blank page.

Weier touches on the composition of *Twelve Poems for Emily Carr* in an interview with Lynnette D'Anna from 1999. His response to the question "What is your relationship to Carr?" is worth quoting at length:

> I like her paintings. They're gorgeous. At some point somebody mentioned to me that she was a writer, she had diaries that were published, so I read those. I just felt that she was a kindred spirit, in terms of her struggle about trying to be an artist while still having to make a living. I felt that she was telling my story. I felt moved by what she'd written, I felt linked, so while I was reading I started taking notes. Phrases, things she'd said. The notes naturally grew into the poems. Most of my writing is diary and a lot of my writing responds to the things I'm reading. It was the most natural thing. (Weier, "Interview" 214)

Weier's passion for Carr makes sense, given that he's also a diarist. So, his poetic response addresses another diarist. After all, the title is *Twelve Poems for Emily Carr*, not "of" or "by" the famous artist. And, while channelling Carr, he must engage with the dilemmas common to all writers of historical fiction: How to represent Carr accurately? How much embellishment to her story is too much? How should he, as a man, reply to the personal reflections of a woman? To Weier's credit and the benefit of the collection, these poems take those questions into account, resulting in meditations on the possibilities of capturing a life in words.

I feel drawn to this place.
From here I can see far into the future.
From here everything looks like prairie;
  everything looks like prairie and home.

After an initial foray into the epistolary format in *Ride the Blue Roan* and *Twelve Poems for Emily Carr*, Weier concentrated on the mode with his second collection of poetry, *Coils of the Yamuna* (1998). These prose poems make up a travelogue of Weier's journey to northern India in the mid-90s. The prologue outlines the process of preparing for the "pilgrimage" to take advantage of "[a]n opportunity" to visit "[m]y two teenage children from a previous marriage [who] were spending a year in the Himalayan foothills with their new blended family." One of the resulting "vignettes," "Old Clothes February 4, 1995," delves into Weier's religious inheritance and a deepening interest in Hinduism. "As a boy I knew little about Hindus," he confesses, "only what I learned from dark and sombre white-skinned missionaries." Weier reports that while in high school, "Mahatma Gandhi, he was a man I admired." Interestingly, he doesn't mention that this admiration was coupled with frustration with Menno Simons' ostensibly pacifist followers. Weier simply had to experience India for himself.

Weier makes it clear this trip is less about comparative mythology than authentic interaction. At a layover at Heathrow in the prose poem "Shame February 5," he considers the implications of "middle-class Westerners" travelling east. Weier volunteers that he and his travelling companion would "insist we're not racist" because they believe all "women and men are equal, deserve equal opportunities, that no one race stands higher than the other," but seeing all the Indian people at the departure lounge gives him pause. He reflects that he feels acutely "self-aware" of being white because he's unsure about how to process that he's part of the minority now: "We see suddenly that racism is not just a belief, but an emotion." As if on cue, the white airline staff pluck Weier and his fellow traveller out of the crowd to offer them a first-class upgrade. As he enjoys Air Canada's finest customer service, Weier thinks "I know why we were chosen" and his "cheeks burn with shame." Self-reflection of that sort is common within Weier's travelogues. Later, when unending rain makes Weier uncomfortable, he understandably grows "restless for the comforts of Canada" and looks to the surroundings to ground him, reporting "[t]he mountains around Mussoorie humble and excite you with their / beauty." Although he has researched India, and even visited previously, he remains a foreigner. It's not the land, but a sense of alienation that inspires Weier's restlessness.

In "Show of Hands February 15," Weier tries to reconcile his foreignness with a lyric poem:

But we haven't come here to buy. We came
to see, to visit, learn. We fear
that India will hate
us for our careful

habits. We are, after all,
rich Westerners.

Later that same day, he enthuses that "I feel drawn to this place. / From here I can see far into the future. / From here everything looks like prairie . . . and home." Weier's acculturation involves a digression into his ornithological interests. In "Bird Brain February 16," he observes "India is almost as crowded / with birds as with people," which appeals to a birder like him. These birds appear "[i]n every puddle. Under every bush. / One hundred species in a few hours." Weier suggests these birds evoke the landscape still "alive with waterholes and slough."

Weier expresses his life-long interest in Hinduism with a numbered series of lyrical poems with the title "Hindu Poet." These poems pose questions about spirituality and muse about possible replies. The first poem begins "Have you seen the Buddha?" (Readers of *Ride the Blue Roan* might answer "maybe?") "Hindu Poet: 3" asks "Did you ever think what non-violence actually means?" (Readers of *After the Revolution* might answer "perhaps?") Each poem in the series ends with an onomatopoeic invocation of the sacred sound in Hinduism ("Om"). In a way, the Hindu Poet poems express curiosity more clearly than Weier's earlier poetry about Mennonite faith. The reason might appear in the final stanza of "Hindu Poet: 6": "Hindus nurture a tolerance that can't be found among Christians. Hindus are happy to practice Hinduism, or Islam, or Christianity, Buddhism. Why not? The goal of all religions is the same." Those lines answer quite a few questions, the least of which is that Hinduism can represent an alternative to Western hypocrisy. Still, *The Coils of Yamuna* ends on an unresolved note. In "First Appendix," Weier notes that "at home, here in my own room, months later I begin to see India more clearly. I begin to see change, take the time to compare an old memory to a young one."

Regarding travel, interviewer Lynette D'Anna posed this question to Weier: "You spend more time than the average person in other countries. How do you think that impacts on your world view and on your writing?"

I feel it's really unfair to write about another country. . . . I go there for three weeks, I write about it, but I know nothing really, I don't know that country. The key for me has been to realize that. . . . I didn't write about India at all, I wrote about myself in India, much more about myself than about India, wrote about myself in another country, put all my weakness and prejudice and bias on display. (210)

In *Coils of the Yamuna*, Weier the diarist realizes that he travelled across an ocean only to find that he couldn't leave the West behind.

——————

> *how do you build*
> *sound   the tone of*
> *Stradivari*

The poem that opens *Violinmaker's Lament* (2002) exposes a new aspect of the poet's persona—psychological uncertainty. The prose poem "Violinmaker January 23, 1997" returns to the issue of labour, but this time a real sense of self-doubt emerges. The speaker uses the epistolary mode to reveal that "I feel . . . like an impostor   feel / like a fake   a fraud   quack doctor on the TV news." The very thought of "repair[ing] a million-dollar Strad" is so disquieting that the fear "someday / someone will find out" he is a phony causes him to "turn and twist at night." Simultaneously dredging and emptying his subconscious in this way, the speaker experiences time slowing down and hears "a clock   in / the other room   now   I think I hear the seconds falling." The punctuation has disappeared, almost as though the poem is an imposition of words onto an empty space. The emptiness itself demands a longer pause than a comma and a deeper silence than a period. As a result, the reader almost endures anxiety alongside the speaker. That does not stop the speaker of the next poem, "How to care for your violin in Winnipeg" from flaunting a depth of knowledge. The poem was originally subtitled "(if you really must move there)" to convey just enough self-aware humour to undercut the wisenheimer mood. The speaker offers six pieces of cheeky advice for prospective Winnipeggers who play the violin or ply the luthier trade. To describe the harsh environmental risks, the speaker draws on another of Weier's preoccupations: birding. "The violin has many enemies," the speaker warns, "Like the wolf, or the peregrine, like the prothonotary warbler, your violin needs love and protection if it's to survive."

Interestingly, the list ends with a metaphor that is both predator and prey. Either Winnipeg is wolf or falcon and the violin a songbird, or the wolf or falcon is the violin, prey endangered by predatory humans.

The idea of an intimidating violin reappears in "Two-million-dollar Strad," only this time it's a profound object of attention. The speaker begins the poem by asserting "the trouble / with old fiddles is this / they're old," and it's possible to verify this claim by peering inside. By comparison, "open a hundred violins / by Stradivari   you'll see cracks and / worm holes," but you'll also spot evidence of repair: "there's more / new wood and glue / than old wood." The difference between the old fiddle and a Strad is the care afforded them. The issue with this small Ship of Theseus (the mythological ship built for King Theseus that was rebuilt after years of maintenance, so Greek philosophers question if it's the same ship it once was) is whether "new wood and glue" convey the requisite "resonant qualities." The poem ends with an analogy to "modern / poems and / poets." Presumably, modern poetry is grafted onto the old masters, but who is to say whether modern poets have produced work as sonorous as their predecessors. In "Tone poem," Weier asks how to produce language that resonates among the emotions. The first two lines double up on verbs: "how do you build / sound   the tone of / Stradivari." The first verb is the domain of the luthier, the second of the violinist. Both terms, though, apply to the poet who strives to induce a vibrant noise with an awkward instrument. As Weier asks in "Diary," "do I pretend to be the Stradivari of words?" To do so, it takes a willingness to break himself down, look closely over the parts, and piece himself back together again. According to "Secrets of Stradivari: The best violin," every luthier knows "the tone of a violin is most easily improved by breaking / the violin into tiny pieces and having it glued / together again by a good workman." It is likely that we're dealing with irony here, and this isn't really a secret of the Stradivari, but the practice of the artisan is what really matters. It's said a good workman never blames the tools for the faults of their work. What's not said is the worker is good because they address their faults before getting to work.

Although the value of the violinmaker's work is unquestionable, the cost appears to be incalculable. Weier's prose poem "Art of lutherie" attempts to account for "long-term or short-term illness and death" that result from working in the profession. The luthier reports enduring "prolonged exposure to dust particles" from wood fibres, which "may result in respiratory / ailments" along with a list of other side-effects as long as a pharmaceutical warning label. Additionally, "modern / glues often contain cancer-causing agents." As any Romantic poet would tell you, art requires suffering, the question is whether that burden is too much to bear. Further, as Weier writes in "Mistakes / November 17, 1982," the wages for that labour is loneliness: "1. I / 2. am a / 3. lonely man" and "I / 7. am a lonely man   made so / 6. many mistakes." Given that "4. all my wives have / 5. left me   they've run off / 6. with my apprentices," the speaker wallows, worrying that "even / 3. my friends want / 2. to cheat / 1. me." Loneliness is suffering that doesn't produce art. At best, it results in emotions more like that other definition of suffering, empathy, which makes the sufferer feel for others. The violin-maker, then, laments the state of loneliness in the world.

<center>~~~~~~~~</center>

> *What does this mean, this lifelong craving,*
> *this longing for words?*

Birds emerged in Weier's poetry with the swallows in *Ride the Blue Roan*, but they become more prominent in his later work. Although the South African travelogue *Under the Wings of Africa* (2007) is mostly composed of prose that records a visit to South Africa with the narrator's spouse, a series of poems disrupts the narrative. Whether this narrative is fictional or not is slyly addressed in Weier's provocative Introduction:

> How much of the story is true? you ask. You're asking me? Yes, I'll leave aside all deception. The story is true. It's all true, for me; every word of this chronicle true. Even the lies are true. (8-9)

The poems, which go by the title "Thunderbird," capture the elicit encounters of an extramarital affair. The third poem, for example, documents the feel of a lover's skin and hair which produces "hard! desire!" but ends the moment "she's gone." The speaker compares "this absence" as "a test," producing a "holy / catechism- / clysm" that is simultaneously disciplinary and disastrous: the former because it taught the speaker about longing, and the

xxxii

latter because it results in loss. The poem concludes with a line about how the affair ended in acrimony: "(and tell me this / how did you earn the right / to judge me?)." The fourth "Thunderbird" similarly contains the refrain "she's gone." The poem "Bird Has Flown" aligns the purpose for the trip, bird watching, with the outcome, the dissolution of a marriage. Just who is the "bird" of the title remains unclear. The subject of the poem, desire, applies to sex and articulation simultaneously: "I opened my // mouth but no word sounded. Only my aching stumbling tongue." The same organ that stimulates arousal also illustrates loneliness. The speaker is a poet at a loss: "What does this mean, this lifelong craving, this longing for words?"

earth
    blue green
    planet   our home
the loss of it
    loss of all this
and love flown
    hourglass sand
    snow sting sand
    ethiopian sand falling

Following his travels to India and South Africa, Weier writes about travelling solo to Australia and Ethiopia in his fourth poetry collection *Where Calling Birds Gather* (2013). What separates this travelogue from the earlier examples is its unique structure. The book is made up of numbered movements and parts, something like a musical composition. Further organization occurs by topic; for example, the first "Argument" poem relates to subsequent "Argument" poems. When the "tourist" in "1.8 Argument" tells the "officer" that he's a "birdwatcher," the officer offers advice on how to find the cassowary. By "3.6 Argument," the tourist, now identified as lower-cased "weier," becomes the butt of a joke when he goes to pick up some groceries: "grocer: why did cassowary cross the road / shopper: see if she could find a tourist." That dialogue weaves through the text until "12.3 Argument," subtitled "(letter to the editor)," where weier writes that he has "not / observed any living cassowary in all my thirty days / sojourn in queensland." By this last section, weier cracks wise, offering a thesis that

i believe cassowary to be an illusion
(barn owl and honey fungus ignis fatuus) created by
a covetous collection of governments anxious to lure
unsuspecting foreigners to provincial resort towns
and villages

The argument is unexpected, but this is not the only surprising move in the collection.

Given the title "Tablature," one might expect this sequence to contain a sort of musical notation, but the poems note features of the Ethiopian flora and fauna. "2.3 Tablature" introduces the African goshawk, which "in circles yowls / whorls the way / it straddles." The poem ends with a remarkable comparison: the speaker notes the "chanting / goshawk the way / it slides" in a journal that he compares to the psalms, stating "six / psalms to go." The psalms, of course, are words to accompany music, only we do not know the tune. Tablature contains the notes, only we do not know the accompanying music. As a result of this silence, the words stir contemplation. "9.3 Tablature" mentions "eighty-five / psalms" in a poem interpreting the movements of several birds weier observed in Ethiopia. For example, the African sacred ibis "sways / at the tip / of a spindle / juniper," the Abyssinian white-eye "flutters in the spray / from a leaky green / garden hose," and the brown-rumped seedeater "scratch / scratch / scratches at the dust" in a manner that "mimics / the un-/ common / house sparrow." The last species listed is notable since it shows up twice in the Book of Psalms (in 84:3 and 102:7 in the King James Version).

The surprise in "12.4 Tablature" for the birdwatchers in the crowd is that it is hard to spot the bird in the poem. Instead, we read about "the language of angels," including "their breath / the rush of wings." The speaker ponders what follows the loss of "earth / blue green / planet   our home" as time slips by like "hourglass sand / snow sting sand / ethiopian sand falling." But it is more complicated than that: "irretrievable irresistible / angels" appear on the planet in the form of the common ringed plover. Both the sparrow and the plover, like the swallow, are common birds that demonstrate the familiarity of beauty. Speaking to D'Anna, Weier expands upon his approach to birding:

I have no desire to control the birds I name. But I do come to know them by naming them. If I name a certain sparrow, study it, look it up in a book, I really learn to see it. I see its features, I learn its habits and learn its call. ("Interview" 212)

What's more, he feels "intimacy and pleasure" from that sort of familiarity (212). It allows him to respond to nature's beauty, and provides a feeling of community, even if the feeling moves in only one direction.

Weier logs the motivation for his travels in the sequence titled "Prairie Tale." "1.2" takes weier from "winter winnipeg," the land of "double digit cold thirties frigid forties" to the city of "addis ababa" with its "double digit thirties fiery forties" to welcome him. While "riding the back roads of australia" in "3.2 Prairie Tale," weier casts his mind around the globe to consider "his children's lives   though now / they're grown he could surely stop / calling them children   but what to call / them instead." On "this sun rainy day" he wonders about their quotidian experiences of "dishes / or laundry or paint," at work or at home, in the present and the future. The final "Prairie Tale," numbered "11.7," relates an anecdote "in the loo at the airport in addis ababa" as "two / twenties boy men bluster above their urinals." The speaker overhears conversation about snow: one mentions the "five feet we had in / january eight years ago" and the other counters with the "fifteen feet snow / in one day . . . / last year." While he "rests on his porcelain / throne," Weier compares the two to "prairie // old-timers" before feeling self-conscious "(sure / he's the old-timer eaves- / dropping)" and

<blockquote>

scribbles
the words
in his notebook
home
he writes
that's home for you

</blockquote>

One reality of Weier's poetry is that his speakers can be outspoken, and it's hard to tell what they truly believe, or what the reader in turn is expected to believe. Although they tend to be frank, and occasionally disagreeable, these personas are difficult to pin down, which is why they're such engaging conversationalists. The Weier Experience involves squinting skeptically at a line or two before nodding along agreeably for a few and ending the poem with an involuntary *huh*. It's a two-step of incredulity and hard-won credibility. In his poetry, Weier prompts the reader to listen closely, consider the positions of his dramatis personae, and make common cause with his speakers. The poems present multiple, sometimes contradictory selves that share some key features. In his 2014 lecture, "Six Mennonite Stories; or, the Plough and the Poet; or What the Skunk Said," Weier presents something of a pseudo-poetics that compares cultivating memories to the construction of self, suggesting that both involve fabulation or, perhaps, fabrication:

> We construct our lives from memories. And, much as we enjoy the cascade of images, talking to siblings about family history often causes trouble. Sometimes memory leads us where we'd rather not go. We notice how our stories have become misshapen. (204)

It follows that memory's faulty so we find a way to fill the gaps somehow. Later in that essay, Weier asserts that telling stories is how we try to order our lives, a process that always involves some degree of invention. Weier relates this idea to the biblical notion translated as the "dominion" over creation that Adam and Eve exerted when they used language to name all the animals on earth. That idea, he contends, applies to writing in that the writer uses names to make sense of things. The reader of Weier's poetry must do their bit as well, coming to terms with what it's like to explore this enigmatic, partly fabulated world and, in turn, looking for the words that might explain our response.

Ahmed, Sara. *The Cultural Politics of Emotion*, 2nd ed., Edinburgh University Press, 2014.

Adorno, Theodor. "Theories on the Origin of Art." *Aesthetic Theory*, edited by Gretel Adorno and Rolf Tiedemann. Translated by Robert Hullot-Kentor, University of Minnesota Press, 1997, pp. 325–331.

Berlant, Lauren. *On the Inconvenience of Other People*. Duke University Press, 2022.

D'Anna, Lynnette. "'Writing is about self-discovery': An Interview with John Weier." *Prairie Fire*, vol. 20, no. 3, 1999, pp. 208–215.

Ngai, Sianne. *Ugly Feelings*. Harvard University Press, 2005.

Weier, John. *After the Revolution*. Turnstone, 1986.

---. *Coils of the Yamuna*. Broken Jaw, 1998.

---. *Ride the Blue Roan*. Turnstone, 1988.

---. "Six Mennonite Stories; or, the Plough and the Poet; or, What the Skunk Said." *The Conrad Grebel Review*, vol. 33, no. 2, 2015, pp. 202-207.

---. *Twelve Poems for Emily Carr*. Punchpenny, 1996.

---. *Under the Wings of Africa*. Wolsak and Wynn, 2007.

---. *Violinmaker's Lament*. Wolsak and Wynn, 2002.

---. *Where Calling Birds Gather*. Turnstone, 2013.

---. "Where Am I Now? Or Why I Am Not a Mennonite." *Mennonite Mirror*, vol. 18, no. 5., 1989, p. 26.

from *After the Revolution*
(1986)

seven acres

not much of a farm when you've grown up on the prairies   but for my
dad and me   planting trees by hand   measuring   marking   digging
spade by blistering spade   keeping a straight line   sharp eye   filling
digging   filling   tree after tree   row after row   cherry   peach   plum
it's big enough

father

my father
the blacksmith works
at his anvil   heats
hammers   heats
again   passing
his hands through
the flames   hair
on his arms
barely singed   he
doesn't fear
the fire   knows
it helps shape
the iron

black and white

1.

it is sunday afternoon

2.

the boy   sits
                at the dining room table

        doesn't look intent
            or interested   simply
        occupied

        is alone

his parents   are in the living (?)
            room

mother   on the couch knitting
            stockings
        only looking
                up
        when he stands
            in the doorway

father   asleep
                in the corner chair
          careful
              not to feel
        its softness

the house   seems empty

his brother   and sisters
                  are either hiding
          in their rooms
             or
       have left

3.

the boy's
        new colouring book
           lies
              open
        in front of him

its pages
    filled
        with the smell
        of sweat soaked
        leather with
        brown and white
        cattle frightened
        and bawling through
        the dust and smoke
        the back and forth

of horses   hides
glistening   while
their riders
lean and sway
under soft felt
and red bandanna

the boy wishes
            he could have been
        a cowboy

4.

the boy
            is colouring
    he works carefully
            yet
    something isn't
                right
he wishes
            his sister
    would come   maybe
        if she helped him
                choose
        the colours
    or
            if his father
    would tell him
            it was
        pretty

he presses
        harder
                the colours
    pale   is it
       the crayons

the boy sits
        back in his chair

the picture isn't done

5.

soon it will be evening

After the Revolution

It's cold outside. He's been dozing in the quiet of his living room, a book open on the couch beside him. He hasn't seen, or even thought of her, for at least ten years and has no idea why she's suddenly appeared. She was a friendly woman. Her eyes, the movement of her hair, the quick smile, her whole body announcing a childlike enthusiasm.

She was a member of the Canadian Communist Party and would be working at a local Marxist bookstore until the Party decided she might be of more use elsewhere. In her spare time she listened to Pete Seeger records and, on occasion, met with her folk friends to play music.

She was a fiddler. She'd come down to his basement shop to have her violin repaired, and they'd spent hours talking about music, about books they liked and fantasy vacations. They'd laughed a lot. It wasn't possible to get together very often, but when they did, they usually went for coffee, and sometimes, up to her apartment on Balmoral.

They'd come to know each other well. She slept, ate and breathed the revolution, and never doubted how good life would be afterwards. She knew he wanted nothing more than a chance to work with an accomplished violin maker. Once, she'd vaulted out of bed, body tensed with excitement saying, "John, after the revolution I'll make sure you're sent to Europe, no, to Italy, to study with the world's best violin experts."

He sits up and reaches for his book. Her revolution seems farther away now than it did ten years ago. In the meantime, he's studied with craftsmen in England and Hungary and has established a reputation of his own. He tries to read. Outside the wind is strengthening. It's getting colder.

just like in the pictures

i've gotta get
that job   six figure
salary   benefits falling
from the pockets of a hundred
three-piece suits   i'll buy
the car   the red one
with tigers all around   i think
the woman comes with it

maybe i'll go
to hawaii   the deep blue
sky   roar of the ocean and sun
bleached sand   green palms
waving   my heart sliding
to the song of island
guitars   the welcome
of soft smiles   and the woman

i'll meet her soon   you know
the one   wearing the perfume
that makes me dash off
to buy her flowers
foolishly forgetting
appointments   million dollar
contracts   and my boss
waiting in his office   and

with that special kind of
stocking   you've seen it on tv
her legs would look so long
i'm sure
loving her would last
forever

last poem

i think this
might be the last
poem i ever write
for you don't get
me wrong it's not
that i'm ungrateful
for all the heart-
broken pieces you've
inspired or that i'm
casually putting you
on the shelf god
knows after one
year of this
nonsense it can
hardly be called
casual but quite
frankly i'm getting
a little tired of the
just-friends business
and besides
i recently met
a woman from
paris

the clearing

it's time

i leave
the sunlit prairie   bounded
fields of grain   fenced
pastures   to touch
the forest   dark
poplar oak elm

the trees
are bare   leaves
brown with dying   sleep
where they've
fallen

i enter
the clearing   rest
face down   taste
the damp   my skin
white against
the ground   legs arms
spreading   hands
clutch leaves   fingers
digging into earth   body
melting
into timeless
motion

the evening
of a new moon

from *Ride the Blue Roan*
(1988)

inheritance

out driving this morning i saw swallows, tanned
bellies, dark back and wings shining in the sun.
pocket nests perched against concrete.

years ago, on the russian steppes, swallows lived
in grandfather's barn. my father, still a boy, waited
for them in spring. the first swallow meant he could
leave his shoes behind for summer, let his toes
wander in the dust. he watched them gather mud
to build their nests. saw the hungry little mouths,
awkward wingbeats turn to adult flight. then suddenly,
missed them, gone in fall.

our old barn in niagara had plenty of openings big
enough for nesting swallows to enter. but when we
built the new one, doors had to be left open all spring
and summer. if the season was dry i had to carry
water, make mud for their nests.

this morning, as we cross the misericordia bridge,
they still hover near their young, slide through air
filled with chattering song. my son and daughter
wonder what they're called.

father the rain and i

midday
a dark sky
it's raining
large drops parachute to earth
the wind has stopped
i stand at the open door of the barn
my father beside me
we have no time no
need for work now
only the rain
watching it fall
large drops
to the earth
no wind
no thought
of danger to crops
those thoughts have fled
hold no meaning
only the rain my father and i
the rain smell the air
only watching the pleasure of the rain
father and i
in our cocoon
he stands beside me
the air around us silk and warm
rain touches the earth

childhood and russia

1.

his mother's russia
was a terrible place
full of things not
to be remembered
　　she never spoke of it

her mother dying when she was two. an ordinary
illness. her father when she was four, some say a
broken heart. the children went to live with their
grandparents. some things aren't easily left behind.
grandfather died before she turned six. he was old.

i wonder if anybody warned her　　she
may not have believed it anyway
it wasn't
believable

during the revolution, now living in the home of her
aunt, his mother watched from a wheat field at night
as her home and village burnt to the ground. in 1926,
the family boarded a ship, they were going to canada.
the aunt's children were buried at sea. his mother, the
stepchild, survived.

canada was the land of hope. still, her first child died
before it was two. after that she spoke often of
heaven, things would be better in heaven.

is there life
after death
so much death

2.

his father, at seventy-six, wakes every morning in
ontario. eats his breakfast. then walks from one end
of the village in russia to the other. past the janzens,
the wiebes, the driedgers. sits on his father's lap,
tugging at his moustache. rides vangka down the
street for the first time, sliding into the mud, as
the big horse turns up the lane. watches the peasants
singing and dancing round the fire after the threshing
is done on his father's farm. goes off to school with
his friends nick and isbrandt. they're laughing.

they were the best
years of his life

3.

what a
beautiful
tragedy

woman talk

1.

a man sits at a table in the cafeteria   obviously
waiting   a woman appears   walking slowly   she's
carrying coffee   their eyes meet   faces soften
no voices   only eyes and faces   smiles   finally
he sips his juice   they talk   laugh together   he
has brought hand-written pages   poems   she
reads   pauses   smiles her reply   reads   he
looks at the rings on her finger   they talk
suddenly she looks at her watch   their eyes shift
voices break   faces fall   she has to go
someone's waiting

2.

the woman smiles an invitation   her thighs are
the whitest he's ever imagined   he's seen them
hiding under her dress   now turns to touch them
soft and trembling to the breath of his caress   lips
erase the final line of hesitation   his mouth
reaching to taste her desire   man's tongue
woman's body   together they speak forgotten
languages   skin on skin   a bath in living water

3.

said she needed some space   time to think   clear
her head   just a few days to herself   he
understood   felt that way himself sometimes   it
wasn't a problem   until this morning   sunday
the waiting is becoming unbearable   why hasn't
she called   what did she mean about space   and

that car parked on the street in front of her house
he won't call her   is reluctant to leave the
apartment   what if she calls and he's not in
the telephone stares at him in silence   he wonders
if it's out of order

hitching post
(for jan)

got into yorkton early sunday afternoon   the others
weren't arriving until later so i decided to go for a
walk   stretch my legs after the trip from regina

thought i saw you drive by   it seemed unlikely   i
knew you hadn't been here since childhood   still
the impression was so strong

and later   walking up and down broadway the sun
warm on my skin   i felt you beside me   showed
you a tie i liked   a car i might someday own   you
laughed   once i almost caught your reflection as we
admired a saddle in the window of the hitching post

yours

buddha and the boat

a few minutes ago i was sitting in my back yard,
now i'm here beside this lake. i'm on the beach.
the waves are large, washing against the shore. it's
a good feeling, the waves and i, nothing else, only
the waves rising and washing within me.

i see a boat. a strange boat, small and wide. a man
stands in it, left hand on the mast. the waves are
loud, i can't hear him, but he beckons sharply. i'm
to join him.

the man is peter. he and i standing in a boat, sailing
in a storm that's been raging for centuries. peter,
with his hand on the mast, face into the wind. the
storm is fierce. perhaps i'm frightened. i wonder if
i'll hear a voice and the water will suddenly be still.

is it really peter? i might be wrong. it could be moses
whose hand is on the mast. no one is steering. why
am i here? why has he taken me? he seems to have no
regard for my safety, doesn't seem to care if i'm
frightened. does he know i am here? i finally ask
where we're going. he says we're sailing. the storm
is too loud, he hasn't heard clearly. why are we
sailing? the wind shrieks. he says yes. he must have
taken me out here for a reason. there's something he
wishes to show me. i ask if he has a message for me.

the waves are large and it's raining. the storm is
fierce. his left hand is firm on the mast. face into the
wind. we're sailing.

in terms of an empty chair

1.

tonight, i'm lonely. i'm no longer sure it's for you.
it's for everyone and no one, everything and
nothing. it simply is.

2.

a teacher of mine thinks that loneliness can best be
described in terms of an empty chair. it's a good idea,
but somehow tonight i can't find a chair large or
strong enough.

3.

in a poem about a forest and lake, a loon and the
stars, i once heard a poet speak the words, *we have
always been lonely*. though neither he nor i have ever
found the line again, i'm sure it's the greatest he's
ever written.

four paintings

he's in an artist's studio. in the corner an easel.
canvases fastened to the walls. on a table, a shoe box
half full of oil sticks, scattered pieces of charcoal,
tubes of acrylic paint, a jar of turpentine, some
brushes.

he's decided to become a painter. in this life he'll
do four paintings.

one is of a large ball of white light. the light
in motion, spinning. as he watches, it envelops
him. his body feels quiet, but fresh.

the second is about colour. bursts of orange, red,
green, yellow, blue. here and there a streak of black.
it's done with a sense of freedom and joy.

another, looks like trees and northern lights. lines of
bright green, vertical, horizontal, dancing, growing
thick and thin. behind the movement of green, empty.

the centre of the last, a shining core of blue. the
colour fading past the edges of the canvas, the same
blue but lighter. or darker. possibly both.

jed

ahead of us jed rides the blue roan   loose in the
saddle body moves with the horse   his hand reaches
up to grab his hat   holds it while twisting to pull a
sweater over his head with the other   god knows
what he's done with the reins   the sweater comes
on but his head can't find a hole   he's caught
there while the roan picks its way across the scree
finally the head appears   and jed's pudgy six year
old hand reaches back for the sandwich packed in his
saddlebag

Footnotes to Dale

8/8/86

i'm sorry i was so angry at you this morning, it's not easy always having you around.

i get along with people best when I'm alone.

12/8/86

when he was four, we played baseball every day. that plastic bat and ball. he was always the batter.

i wonder how he survived that time. my anger, impatience. somehow our game was worthless to me.

four years later it's easier. he's grown up, can catch and throw

and he's forgiven. this morning in the car, i don't know whether to laugh or cry. he's quiet for a long time, looks up at me and says, you know dad, i was born for baseball. quiet again, then, babe ruth and i are sort of the same, you know.

12/10/86

in russia when father was young, he was told to prepare for the trip to canada. the voyage, by sea, would be long and difficult, hard on a boy's stomach. there was a swing hanging from the willow tree. the

best thing he could do, they said, was to spend as
much time swinging as possible. he wasn't seasick
once.

11/1/87

my father used to keep a bag of peanuts on the hot
air-duct in our basement when i was a child. they
were his. still, he always looked a little awkward
when we found him there with his hand in the bag, as
though he wished he hadn't been caught.

he and i have hardly spoken since mother died, and i
gave up my marriage. did you know? the peanut is a
brazilian herb, a member of the pea family. it has
yellow flowers.

31/3/87

you called, said you were afraid your father was
going to die. why are you worried, he probably will.
it's something we carry in our pockets.

once, when jonathan was five, we were out for a
drive. he pointed out the window at a cemetery and
asked what it was. i explained to him that it was
where you buried people after they died. he looked
relieved, said he was glad they had such places. it's
not something you laugh at every day, but his words
caught me by surprise. he said it wouldn't look nice
if dead people were lying around in ditches. don't
you think, he said.

13/4/87

we need to talk about this.

if it's true as you say, that i treat you like a child, then
i suppose you must also treat me like your father. this
is getting complicated. i wish we could just grow
up. but failing that, do you think we could meet? maybe
somewhere in the middle.

26/5/87

at a baseball clinic.

i've thrown the ball. my daughter, intent on some-
thing across the diamond, has crept too close to the
baseline. the throw is bad, pulls far to the left, and
suddenly the world stops. there are hours of silence
as the ball, in slow motion, arches toward her. the
ball twisting and sliding, and i can't even find the
time to pray. i am hot and frozen as it sails by just to
the side of her curly hair

and finally i can breathe again.

14/7/87

baseball and healing. the team, the church, a common
cup, the sacrament of handshake. and just when the
last thing i wanted was to be healed.

from *Twelve Poems for Emily Carr*
(1996)

Journal
January 23, 1930

yesterday I went to town and bought
this book to enter scraps in   this
book   this little book   not a diary
for statistics
and dates
and proper spelling
and happenings
but just to jot me down in   un-
varnished me   old me at fifty-eight
why are we so ashamed of our most
honest parts?

I think it helps to write things
down   to lay them down   on paper
writing helps you
catch things   clarify them
if I don't write thoughts down   where
will they go?

I'll tell you my secrets little book
but listen
never let me write
anything
that's not my own

Journal
September 9, 1933

how
do you
paint sky the
tall tree pushing
the slope in the corner
and pines how
do you paint the world from
Beacon Hill round
small blue dome lid over top
the white cloud's dance.
purple hills and snowcapped
mountain far side of the strait how
do you paint sea sky no
horizon the pink grass leaning
the glass-topped sea and wild lawless
places decay and dank smells the
rotting roots and tangle
growth of jungle the wisdom of old forest
sand arbutus trees how do you paint the
house its rooms children
squalling like gulls over rough
ground brown earth greengrey weeds
the ripple as breeze passes how do you paint
sound wind the roll roar rhythm of
ocean wind some days that's all I hear how do
you paint bracken its exquisite coil squeezed
and bashful white butterflies quivering trees
stretching into new clothes leaves growth how
do you paint that growth the foghorn
the essence of the fuchsia how
do you
paint
that

Journal
April 10, 1932

dear mother earth mother dear earth mother I think
mother I have always belonged always especially mother
dear earth always belonged to you earth mother I have
loved from babyhood dear earth toddling and tumbling
in the garden earth always especially from babyhood
belonged always loved mother to roll upon you earth
since I was a baby loved love little baby roll earth
tumble and toddle to lie dear mother belong with my
face pressed always love earth dear right down
especially always earth mother onto you dear since a
little baby toddle my face pressed always in my sorrow
lie love roll pressed against you tumble I love the earth
look of you press against sorrow mother you love the
look earth mother love the smell you dear smell look
tumble and the feel of you since a baby when I always
belonged die especially mother when I mother die earth
love the smell I should like the feel of you to be in you
uncoffined pressed against die always belonging sorrow
especially the feel love unshrouded earth since
babyhood the petals toddling and tumbling always
petals of flowers against my skin and you dear mother
lie love roll upon you belong in the garden dead
uncoffined petals and earth always love belonged baby
pressed against my flesh and you when I die tumble
earth cover me always up love

Journal
August 16, 1933

today I uncovered *The Mountain*   now I feel sick
sick I feel sick there's   nothing in it one big
terrible canvas I have   painted all
week but caught nothing so then what's the use how do you
paint a mountain a landscape   how
do you look see how do you know
if I could just know that my painting moved
someone or joy gave them joy

sometimes I think I should quit painting
take up charring   housecleaning is not so bad
when you throw your heart into it   I believe
I could shine and polish   perfectly
I've kalsomined four rooms   today ceilings
walls everything clean and   sparkling
the shelves so white they ache
for pots and pans the walls   for pictures

I could have kept house once there was a man
who loved me forty years ago forty years
he still   sends pressed flowers   remembers the girl
who was   twenty do you wish you had he says
he still   needs to know still needs

all that love spent over me and I not able
to return it but men are sometimes so
stupid and he'd have found me
indigestible I'd have found him   boring I wrote
a few poems once I was in love once too

34

Journal
June 24, 1938

there is a place and I am
going there I have seen
it from above below all
around I went there in my
dreams again last night a
deep bay a sandy beach
and driftwood a steep
bank and the twisting
orange and scarlet boles
of beautiful arbutus
trees above that the
pines stretching for the
sky I should like when I
leave this body to float
from here up those
mountain passes to rest
in the silence wonder
curl through the trees I
love the trees trees the
secret's out I am not a
church-goer but I am religious I love
trees I have three new canvases on the
way all of woods they are all woods pictures
they are all of trees

Journal
October 3, 1939

1.

how do you paint
the war the howling
war earth hung
in the balance twisting
from hope to despair the
loss of it

paint ships
crashing across the sea
and planes broken bodies a chorus
of the drowning
people high buildings
hurled smashed
about the sky soldiers
fallen their hot
blood spills   nations
hate
and hiss
and hyper-
ventilate the earth
is hideous
with this roar war
loose
and hustling round it
this horrible

excess I am
afraid
to wake afraid
to fall
asleep

again

2.

     and how do you

           paint

  the peace of this
    cabin

        that ridge

  those tall
firs and smaller
   pines paint

       the rain

         fall rain

            breathe

    leaves swell

         moss

    sip earth

      lips

     buzz wasps

  my paintings

    of the past
     month hold

autumn and
   the most
    unusual joy
   the smaller

       the cage
      the better
        the bird

    sings

Journal
December 31, 1940

have
thoug
ht
about
death
great
deal
this
year
find
the
earth
love
ly
autum
n does
not
disma
y me
anymo
re
than
does
the
early
winte
r of
my
body
I
have
lived

from *Coils of the Yamuna*
(1998)

Time Travel
February 3, 1995

The white-rumped sandpiper, when it starts migration in July, departs the northern shores of Canada, follows the wind south and east across the tundra, along Hudson Bay, then flies from the Maritimes over the Atlantic to South America, not the shortest route, to the southern-most tip of South America, winters way down in Tierra del Fuego. That's a trip of 15,000 kilometres, great hardship, at least one month in spring, two months in fall, feeding and resting and flying. The white-rumped sandpiper makes that trip, back and forth, 30,000 kilometres, to nest in northern Canada each new year.

How does it find its path? What impulse drives it? From the Arctic to the Drake Passage. All that way. I believe it's true, Peter Matthiessen says it's so. Sandpiper. White flash and tail, long wings, I can see it, I carry a memory map of the world inside my head. There. Flying up in August in Alaska. Settling again with its companions along the shores near Cape Horn a few months later. Why shouldn't I believe that? White-rumped sandpiper, wind bird, with its breast muscle, and quick metabolism, and hollow bone. The sandpiper is a bird of wonder and miracle, a bird with all the world as home.

Airport. Air traffic control. 747. Tomorrow my partner and I fly from Toronto halfway around the world to visit in India. East and west, north and south India. How many kilometres is that? And how many hours, really? We'll leave here, fly for 24 hours, arrive there 36 hours later. Can you imagine such peculiar obsessions with time? Far less prepared than the white-rumped sandpiper for our journey, yet so many of them never complete that first travelling cycle.

Basket of plastic and tin, the 747. It takes a certain kind of faith to keep this bird afloat, so high above the speeding ground. The sandpiper is a bird of wonder and miracle and great faith.

Old Clothes
February 4, 1995

The religions of India: Hindu, Muslim, Sikh and Zoroastrian, Buddhist and Jain. The sacred rivers. Those dancing gods and goddesses. A hundred golden temples. All the ancient literatures.

As a boy I knew little about Hindus, only what I learned from dark and sombre white-skinned missionaries. Their talk, their slide shows. That they had gone to India to make Christians out of Hindus. That they dressed them in western clothes and gave them jobs as cooks and drivers. That they splintered families. That they saved Hindus, taught them how to pray. Hindus! Imagine teaching Hindus how to pray! That it was the only way to save them.

I grew up a Mennonite boy. Religion punched and poked into a rucksack, what didn't fit we threw away, like burning old clothes. I tried to keep myself hidden in a corner, I didn't want that Mennonite God to notice me, anyone to notice me. I never argued about it, heaven is something we all wish for, but I couldn't believe that Hindus wouldn't get to heaven on their own. I don't know where I got that notion, I must have been inspired.

Later I developed a more serious interest in Hinduism. Even in high school I'd understood already that my parents' faith was alien to me, and it was frightening. Mahatma Gandhi, he was a man I admired.

Hindu Poet: 1

Have you seen the Buddha? Did you see how he stepped to
his mother's side? Did you see the seven suns, and the skin

of the moon, and the dark cloud? Have you seen the
Buddha? Can you catch his voice? Did he call in the night

to his father? Did he long for a daughter? Would he cry
for his wife and son? Have you seen the Buddha? Did

you see the palace and the dancing women? Do you desire
the women? Did you dance with the women, did you mimic

those mad and dancing women, would you lie with those
women? And the old man. Have you seen the sick man,

the dead man by the road, the corpse in the grass? Did you
talk with your friends about the dead man, naked man,

corpse, the snake in the tall grass? Have you seen the
Buddha? In the forest? Did you see his frame and his fat,

by the fig and the banyan tree? Did you watch with him
for the dusk, through the dark and the wet of the night? Did

you wait for the sun and the dawn? Have you ever seen
the Buddha? Did you hear him shout? Have you counted

the world and the wheel? Have you seen the fire, the
leaping flame and the bone, the pile of bones? Have you

seen the Buddha? If you're ever on the road and chance
to see the Buddha... Ooooooooooommmmmmmmmmm.

Shame
February 5

Heathrow Airport, about racism. Two things. Or maybe three or four.

Susan and I think like most middle-class Westerners, we insist we're not racist. We tell our friends that all women and men are equal, deserve equal opportunities, that no one race stands higher than the other. But suddenly, at Heathrow, we face a departure lounge crowded with Indians. Foreign faces, foreign dress, foreign sounds, foreign colours and smells, a foreign crowd. Dark skins. An introduction to India. No *namaste* and smiling *saried* hostess like in the ads, this 747 will be full of real Indians. I see my surprise catalogued on Susan's face.

What do we feel? Anger. Fear. Isolation. All of those. Self-aware. White. We feel white. We look for other white faces. What did we think, that we were travelling to an India full of North Americans? If India is so poor, how can all these people afford to fly? We see suddenly that racism is not just a belief, but an emotion.

White faces. There. The airline staff, they see us, pull us aside. They think they can give us an upgrade, put us in first-class. Is it because of my tie and jacket, because of Susan's modern skirt? Is it because of my smile, do they like my smile, smiles always look good in first-class. Probably they know that we're *Frequent Flyers*, that we fly Air Canada a dozen times a year. All those reasons for the upgrade.

And we accept the airline's offer, step happily into first-class. Big reclining chairs, lots of space, private tv, meals on white china and wine, hostess hovering with beverages and suggestions. Comfort, luxury. We love our upgrade, our first-class accommodations.

Isn't this great, I say, as our plane leaves the runway. But my cheeks burn with shame, I know why we were chosen. I'm glad my writing colleagues in India can't see me.

Hindu Poet: 3

Did you ever think what non-violence actually means? Do you remember Gandhi and his hundred thousand followers, in the movie, how they stood against the guns and horses and the rushing soldiers? How they lay down, how the horses refused to step on them. Non-violence. A harmless weapon of their own. In South Africa. In India. Fighting for reform. Without guns. They refused to take a life. Do you remember all that? Have you read any of the books?

It's not just cows, you know. North Americans think it's the cows are sacred. North Americans laugh and shake their heads when they talk about India's cows. But here's what I think. Westerners can't even think that far, it's a failure of imagination. It's not just cows. Every speck, and bit, and fleck, and spot of life in India is sacred. Indians believe that every shred of life is blessed and sacred. Can you imagine that? Henry Thoreau would have understood that.

You see monks on the sidewalk, naked except for one careful cloth at the waist, the piece of rag they clutch over their mouths. Holy men. Sweepers swing and sway around them with feathered brooms. Those monks won't step on any living thing; they won't kill an insect by breathing it. Non-violence. Did you ever think what it actually means? Many Indians never eat meat. When you visit in India you'll likely be a tourist vegetarian.

Every spot and bit of life is sacred. You should think about this the next time you slap a mosquito. You could think about it next time the crop duster flies over your house, next time you pass the abattoir on Marion Avenue, if you hear a scream and smell the frightened bloody cattle. Do you ever think how much you depend on the life around you? Do you think of this while eating carrots? Even vegetables were once alive.

Oooooooooooooooooooooooommmmmmmmmmmmmmmmmmmm.

Monkey Mind
February 9

Monkeys thrive in Mussoorie. Rhesus monkeys stroll, sit, watch, mate along the top of the stone wall in the Mussoorie bazaar. Langur monkeys wait in the branches high above the forest floor. Jon says we shouldn't look them in the eye, especially the langurs, they might see it as aggression, they might attack. He says the rhesus monkeys wake him every morning in his dorm. They swing from the trees through the early sun and mist, they crash on the dorm's sheet metal roof, gallop across, and vanish in the trees at the far end of the building. He falls asleep again. Ten minutes. Then they're back. Crash. Gallop. Anna says the langur monkeys are lazy, sometimes they pee on you from up in a tree.

Monkeys with their mates and families scatter all along the forest roads to Rishikesh. A story is told in the ancient literature of the god Hanuman who brought his monkey hosts to help the prince, Rama, in his battle against the evil Ravana. Millions of monkeys, they formed a monkey bridge to the island of Sri Lanka.

The road to Rishikesh. Traffic. I tell Anna that I'm surprised never to see people hurt on the Indian highways, there's so much traffic. She says I should just wait. She says that it happens. She says that if you hit someone with your car on the highway, a pedestrian, that you keep going, you don't dare stop. You drive for your life. She says relatives of the injured or dead pedestrian will wish to kill you. You must remember to hit and run, you better just run, she says.

Jon says the Beatles visited in Rishikesh in the 1960s, dropped from the sky in their helicopter, much too far to drive. He says he read this somewhere, they came to meet some famous yogi.

Under the Weather
February 10

Evening.

After six days in India I already feel restless for the comforts of
Canada. My bed. My furnace. The hot water tank. The bath. The
fridge. Old friends. My sense of adventure seems to stop at this,
I'd like to spend every night at home in my own bed. I feel a bit
like my son, writing:

> Today is my 68th day away from home. I've written
> 42 letters, received eight letters from home, I love
> hearing from home.

Did you weigh the yearning in those three simple numbers? Like
most Westerners I'm committed to the idea of travel, but tonight
I find such a gap between the idea and the travel itself.

I become nervous and irritable, crazy. Susan and I with one of
our teen children every night in this small room. No tv or video-
cassettes to hypnotize us, nothing but a single deck of cards,
nowhere to go. I'd like to crash the walls out.

Wind claps on our sheet metal roof. The sky hangs heavy with
cloud. Leaves whisper. These Himalayan oaks speak much the
same language as the elm trees on Ashburn Street. They gossip
about rain.

Hindu Poet: 4

I love you
I love you in the flowers
I love you in the rose, love you in the tulips and the poppy, love you
        in the fuchsia, the cactus
I love you in the gray tit and the bush-robin, the creeper
I love you in the tiger and the langur
Love you in the stars, in the moon, in the rain and in the cold
I love you in the weather
Yes, I love you in oranges, and in mangoes, and in curry, love you
        even in the rice
Love you in the moss and rocks
Love you on the cliff and in the cave
Love you in the brown, in the green
Love you in the wood and in the water, in the water buffalo
I love you in the minute, in a minute, love you in the year
Love you in the dawn, in the daytime, in the breath and in the life
        and in the light
I love you in the blade and in the bridle
I love you in the pine and in the pyre
I love you in the drum and the violin, the sitar and harmonium, in the
        trumpet and the bass
I love you in the bow and in the arrow
Love you in the bee and in the bean
In the soup and in the honey
Love you in your breasts
Love you in your thighs, in your eyebrows and your eyes, I love you
        in your sex
Love you in your lips and in your skin
Yes, I love you, and I love you, and I love you
Ooooooooooooommmmmmmmmmmm.

Paper Trail
February 12

The mountains around Mussoorie humble and excite you with their
    beauty. Trails trace the life of each hill and valley, side to
    side, up to down, through rock and forest. Some inspired
    environmentalist has tagged a variety of trees; western
    yellow pine, Himalayan cedar, rhododendron, Atlantic cedar.
    Atlantic cedar, how did that get here? I take pleasure in his/
    her forethought, I wish I knew more about trees, find the
    western yellow pine especially beautiful. Long needles and
    coarse scaled bark.

We find eyesores along the trail; garbage dumped in the gullies, red
    and white and blue plastic rustling among the trees. Bill says
    at dinner that India's a filthy place and he tells stories in
    support. I'm confused and upset about this, feel that as a
    visitor I shouldn't notice ugliness. And anyway, there's
    garbage in Canadian forests.

We meet Indians, four men with pick and shovel and mortar out to
    repair the trail, and a woman gathering brush for firewood.
    We meet donkeys carrying loads and a donkey driver. Many
    of the households in the region receive their deliveries on
    donkeys. One Jersey-coloured cow feeds and gongs on the
    hillside.

They say that during summer monsoon this forest fills with wild
    flowers, that orchids hang from every tree.

Hindu Poet: 5

Having read pages and pages of ancient literature, the Puranas, the
        Mahabharata, the Yoga-sutras;

Having read about the terror brought by powerful rajas, about deceit
        and greed and dissension, about a variety of evil omens,
        calves not sucking, cows not giving milk, horses weeping,
        having read regarding images of gods and goddesses
        sweating from fear;

Having read about killing and war, about oceans and mountains,
        swords, horses and chariots, about wealth, golden bracelets
        and earrings, about Krishna's sixteen thousand wives;

Having read about ritual and sacrifice, about spider and snake bite,
        about the holy waters of the Ganga, about singing birds and
        bright flowers, lust and playfulness;

About the mango and the apple, about nature and time, about sky
        and earth and fire;

Having read about elements and elephants; about long hair and
        navels, about sun and moon and metamorphosis;

Having read about incarnations, about incantations, about holy men,
        their dreams and prayers and devotion, about monkey-gods
        and elephant-gods, about a black and angry goddess;

It still all sounds foreign to me. I haven't found one mention of
        weather. Not one word about the cold in the hills in winter.
        Not a hint about the summer heat. Not one rune about the
        rhythm of rain, the moment of the monsoon, momentum of
        the monsoon.

Oooooooooooooooooooooommmmmmmmmmmm.

Riddle
February 15, 1995

The contradictions of ugliness and beauty, poverty and wealth. The
        Taj Mahal, its garden, flowers, green trees, ponds; its birds,
        rose-ringed parakeet and Indian roller; its white marble dome
        and sunrise; its mountains of rock inlaid in semi-precious
        stone; its gates and minarets. But just outside those gates, the
        dogs and beggars, their maimed bodies.

The Yamuna River behind the Taj lies stagnant and dirty, banks litter
        with garbage, swarm with varieties of vultures and kites and
        crows. Two painted storks dabble knee-deep in the water,
        sandpipers race along the mud flat, black-winged stilts stretch
        their awkward legs. Ruddy shelducks float and preen. Egrets
        flap and sail, flap and sail.

Shah Jahan, what does that name inspire? This tomb took 20 years
        and 20,000 men to build. And one favourite wife. I've
        checked the calculations of Sam Clemens on his world tour,
        and I've spoken to his Satan.

Order. Balance. Symmetry. Matching ponds and minarets. Two
        bodies, man and woman, lovers. Perfect squares and circles
        crumbling, tumbling into turmoil.

It's the threat of anarchy that frightens me. In the stones and
        buildings. On the highway. In the market. Caught in that
        angry crowd in Meerut. Demons of death and disorder steal
        the arms, legs, bodies, lives of Indian animals and people.

Show of Hands
February 15

Craftsmen,
and women, their dazzling
creations. So many
people here still working
with their hands.

A treadle sanding wheel, an orange slip
of stone chased into a petal. Warp and weft,
wool and shuttle. Chisel, graver, handsaw
and file. Knife, awl, hammer.
Fire. Tong and plier. Paint
and brush. One long bolt of quiet
cloth, a wooden block design, kitchen
saucer full of dye and one young man
at work. Dip and stamp.

Craftswomen, craftsmen, the beauty
of their hands and eyes, their work.

Marble box, Sahib? Handmade
silk, Sahib? One
green carpet, Sahib? Would you like
to buy, Sahib?

But we haven't come to buy. We came
to see, to visit, learn. We fear
that India will hate
us for our careful
habits. We are, after all,
rich Westerners.

Home Stretch
February 15

Except for the big gates, the walls, the palaces.
Except for the turrets and domes, the balconies,
      the treasury building,
       the armoury and banquet hall.
Except for the acres and acres of carved stone.
Except for the chambers and hidden corridors for Akbar's
      one thousand concubines.
Except for red flowers, bougainvillea,
      and the hot sun in February.
Except for an Indian chat, brown bird that flies from perch
      to perch, and the bright saried and suited young
      women from a Madras girls' school picnicking on
      the lawn.

Fatehpur Sikri.
Deserted city.
City of dry wells.
City without water, Akbar's affront.
Balanced on a green hill above the plain.

I feel drawn to this place.
From here I can see far into the future.
From here everything looks like prairie,
      everything looks like prairie and home.

Hindu Poet: 6

Hindus feel strongly about their religion. They visit their temples weekly and on holy days to bow before the symbols of their gods. They keep small shrines for worship in their homes. Taxi and bus drivers carry images and flower garlands on their dashboards, they burn incense in their vehicles.

Hindus worship. They pray, they repeat mantras, they read scriptures. They bring offerings of flowers, rice, rupees. Hindu temples cluster with images, gods and goddesses. Krishna, Rama, Parvati, Shiva, Vishnu, Lakshmi, Kali, Brahma, Sita, Indra. There are gods for everyone, for every occasion, plenty of gods to go around, no one needs to feel left out.

Huge crowds of worshippers gather for religious festivals, millions of worshippers. They meet to commemorate events in the lives of favourite divinities. They make regular pilgrimages to holy rivers, the Ganges, or to other holy sites.

Some Hindus leave their everyday lives. They become ascetics and wander off into the forest, or the mountains, where they sit cross-legged, and sleep on the ground, and fast, and seek salvation.

Hindus are no more idolaters than Christians. They speak of the symbolic nature of their many descriptions of god.

Yet Hindus nurture a tolerance that can't be found among Christians. Hindus are happy to practise Hinduism, or Islam, or Christianity, Buddhism. Why not? The goal of all religions is the same. Different creeds, they say, only depict different paths to the same god. God may possess disparate forms, and names, and apparent contradictions, and still be one god. Hindus feel strongly about their religion.

Ooooooooooooooooommmmmmmmmmmmmmmmm.

Bird Brain
February 16

India seems almost as crowded
with birds as with people. The
landscape yesterday and today
alive with waterholes and slough,
not yet perfectly flat and drained
like the farmland south and west
of Winnipeg. Call it progress,

advances in farm technology.
Indian birds everywhere here in
Bharatpur. Acres of forest and marsh.
More birds than Susan and I imagined.
In every puddle. Under every bush.
One hundred species in a few hours.

India is crowded. With birds. And with
people. Must be as many birds as people.

Hindu Poet: 9

The holy river Ganga, the goddess Ganga, she flows from the
       Himalayas, flows from the snow and the evergreen trees,
       born from the cold and the mountains;
The roaring river Ganga, falls through deep gorges, rattles through
       chasms and canyons;
The goddess Ganga, whom Hindus worship, whom Hindus flock
       to honour and worship, where Hindus bathe and Hindus
       gather, where Hindus drink;
The mother Ganga, the millions of pilgrims to Ganga, pilgrims
       who die on the shores of the Ganga, whose ashes scatter
       in the Ganga, half-burned bodies floating in the Ganga,
       sadhus' bodies tied to rocks and drowned in the Ganga;
Holy river Ganga, river of the Indian people, river of Indian
       history, river of rajas and moguls, river of poor and of
       peasant, defeat and victory; Mother Ganga, river of moods
       and seasons, river that winds lazy through plains, river of
       desert, it dries into desert;
The Goddess Ganga, river of monsoon, river that rises and rises,
       river that floods, raging river, river that ravages village and
       hut, carries down cattle, and crops, Mother Goddess
       Ganga;
Holy Mother Ganga, giver of nourishment and death, giver of
       fertile silt and erosion, river that runs deep into the sea,
       river that washes chemical waste into the sea, river that
       washes the waste from distilleries, refineries, factories;
       cyanide, arsenic, lead, zinc, selenium, chromium, mercury,
       cadmium, phosphorus, nitrogen sulphate, carries them far
       into the sea;
The holy river Ganga, har har Ganga, hai Ganga, dearest Ganga,
       Oooooooooooommmmmmmmmmmmmmmmmmmmmmm.

Malaise
February 23

All our
fears about
illness. We

drink
only tea
or mineral water.
Never
eat raw
vegetables. Eat no
meat. Never
miss
our malaria
pills. Hundred

dollars worth
of pills and saw
no more than
two
or three
mosquitoes. We

haven't
been sick
once.

Open Season
March 13, 1995

The sun sets in the evening, wakes again
each morning. The moon follows. Wind
swirls and howls over hills, through
trees, round corners. Rain
scorns all fences, all boundaries.
Red-tailed hawk pairs, after migration,

return to the same nest year
after year. They renovate; add
a few twigs, branches, dried
grass. That Baltimore
oriole stops at the same
neighbour's backyard every

spring. If its nectar jar
isn't swinging from the clothesline,
it teeters, whistles, scolds, dips
its head till the homeowner
notices. I have found no
good reason for my preoccupations

with India, what brought me there,
when I will return, I'm sure now
that I'll return. The sun falls
in the evening. Wakes
again. The moon chases. Wind
swirls over hills, through trees.

Rain ignores all boundaries, scorns
even these established boundaries.

First Appendix

Our Indian acquaintances get excited when they learn that I visited India 20 years ago. They want to know how things have changed. You must observe many changes, they say. How would you say India has changed.

To be honest, I don't notice many changes. India doesn't look that different after all these years. I see a few newer cars; the Suzuki Maruti looks new, looks like a car you might see in 1995 in North America. The other cars, the buses, trucks, motorcycles taxis, they look just like in 1975. The landscape looks the same. The people look the same, their dress. The Taj Mahal looks the same. But that's not the answer our hosts want to hear.

It's hard to compare one time and place to another. Maybe if we'd landed in Calcutta like I did the first time, if we'd retraced every step. Maybe if we'd travelled ordinary class. Maybe if the temperatures had stretched into the 40s. Or if we'd stayed longer. Maybe I've changed too much. I try to give the right answers, I want to be a good guest, I want Indian people to like me. Eventually, my examiners offer the words they'd like to hear. Industry, population, pollution, they say. So many changes.

Here at home, here in my own room months later, I begin to see India more clearly. I begin to see change, take the time to compare an old memory to a young one.

from *Violinmaker's Lament*
(2002)

Violinmaker
January 23, 1977

possessed with violins my violins I am notice every flaw
every scratch a nick a lump in the purfling this corner
almost a half millimetre longer than the other the new
varnish smudged here on the heel haunted by violins think
about them at night lie awake far into the night and bother
about my violins possessed obsessed bedevilled

by violins impostor I feel like that like an impostor feel
like a fake a fraud quack doctor on the tv news what do
you know about violins where did you study who are you
to be charging two months' salary for a hand-built new
violin who are you to repair a million-dollar Strad someday
someone will find out turn and twist at night throw the
covers off so hot and sweating someday I know some
player will drag me to jail for the price of a violin minutes

pass so slowly in the dark hours drag open my eyes check
the time again lie awake in bed beside Sara hear the sound
of her breathing in out she seems to sleep so peacefully
all my wives have slept so peacefully how did they manage
that there a rafter snaps in the frost of this Scarborough
winter night cold night somewhere a tap drips a clock in
the other room now I think I hear the seconds falling

How to care for your violin in Winnipeg

1. Never leave your violin in a parked car in summer! You've heard the stories about dogs suffocating in hot cars. You might as well drop your violin in a pot on the stove. The sun will heat the inside of the car and the glue that holds the pieces of wood together will soften. Your violin will sigh and twist into remarkable new configurations.

2. Be careful in winter too! Homes get very dry in the Winnipeg winter. Violins, when they dry, will shrink and crack. Houseplants help keep the atmosphere moist and friendly. It's important to shower every day. That keeps you clean, keeps your lover happy, and puts moisture in the air. Don't take the violin in the shower with you!

3. Never leave your precious Strad lying in the living room on your new blue Bauhaus couch! Someone is sure to come and sit on it. This is especially true on the day of a wedding or a big party.

4. Don't place the violin case on the driveway while you lift the beer and groceries out of the trunk! Your car may slip out of park and roll over the violin. Worse. You may realise you forgot to buy the beer and drive over the violin on your way back downtown to visit the beer store.

5. Be sure to keep your violin away from your partner when you come home from a party late at night! Many an unsuspecting instrument has been hurtled against the fridge, or smashed over its owner's right shoulder by a husband or wife angry about spending another evening home alone washing and folding the laundry.

6. Be careful of flood and fire! Check the height of the river as you cross the bridge. Flick the oven elements to *off* when you leave the house. Ask yourself: Is my neighbour burning the stubble or the leaves? The violin has many enemies. Like the wolf, or the peregrine, like the prothonotary warbler, your violin needs love and protection if it's to survive.

Tool talk

whisper
of the jack
plane   murmur
of chisel
and gouge
grumble

of the drill   a sobbing
file   sandpaper
complaint
hiss
of scraper
spit
of bending iron
the censorship

of clamps
a handsaw
growl
barking hammer
scream of resaw
the jointer wails
router shrieks   the
quiet waiting wood
language of hand

and wood and tool
a wooden
speech
wood'en
talk
if I were you

Violinmaker
September 12

lazy sit in the shop late into
the morning no work in me drink
coffee the radio a cigarette
from the pack Sara keeps in the freezer
smoke curling
front door opens what

now nothing in the daybook never
see clients in the morning a visitor
beggar one of the street
people what does he want a dollar
two dollars twenty-five cents
he really asks so little
takes it thank you and goes

leaves me to wonder about
the line between us him and me
scratched in the sand
the difference similarity
the line that joins us in this world
when nine men/women get a job
the tenth must stay hungry must

live in the alley rules of the game
those lessons of youth
hunger revolution civil war
these three always packaged
together violin
and bow
and string

Diary

why do people keep diaries?
why do I?
what's the purpose of this diary?

    a. a diary simply marks the passage of time,
          my time (from nothing to nothing again)

    b. diaries are always full of sorrow and struggle, diarists
          (myself included?) wish to chronicle their
          unhappiness for all the world to see

    c. some people feel that writing things down, laying them on
          paper, will absolve them. I desire absolution

    d. the Cremonese diary, a story of war and pillage and
          plunder, and starvation, a story of plague,
          sixty thousand children burned in the local
          crematorium, a history of the violin

    e. maybe the diary will be my ticket to immortality, have you
          ever seen a violinmaker's diary? did any of the Amati family
          keep a diary? did Jakob Stainer? This might be the first

    f. do I pretend to be the Stradivari of words?

    g. maybe someday my children will wish to find me. Doug in
          Syracuse, Sandy in Tel Aviv, John in L.A. a small hope.
          someday my children will try to reach me. who was our
          father? where is he? I will write this map to guide them

    h. why can't I write anything happy

Violinmaker: Riddle

so many things I don't understand things I puzzle about
need to ask

how did the shape of the violin ever come to be was it
someone's idea did someone think of it at breakfast was it
just coincidence who created the design with all those
curls and scrolls points and corners how could you dream
that up

one hundred years from now will there still be wood for
violins will there still be spruce forest and maple what
will happen to ebony will all the rainforests be gone

one hundred years from now will they build violins from
plastic will they play Mozart on synthetic Strads will they
only build synthesizers

where have all my wives gone are they happy without me
am I happy building violins

the women at the go-go centre on Danforth Avenue with
their naked breasts and thighs what do they think about
while they take their clothes off why would they do it
what do they mean do they like me to see them that way

when will the messiah finally come what happens then

Secrets of Stradivari: The best violin

1. violins should be made up of fibres of different lengths so
    as to have one fibre of a size to suit every note in the
    compass of the instrument

2. the tone of a violin is most easily improved by breaking
    the violin into tiny pieces and having it glued
    together again by a good workman

3. if you prefer, the same good workman could simply glue
    up a new violin out of a few thousand toothpicks

4. the wisdom of Monsieur Maupertuis, 1724

5. ha-ha-ha (it might be simpler just to play the individual
    toothpicks)

6. (why not workwoman)

Silk

happy tonight
two coats of varnish
golden brown
brushed on today
no puddles no runs
smooth
just right

just right
smooth
no runs or puddles
brushed on today
golden brown varnish
two coats
tonight happy

By plane to Minneapolis

I love tools
love the feel of tools
        their weight balance and my skin
I love the look of tools bench-light
        on cold blue steel
        warm wood handles
I love to study how
        tools are made and where
        by whom (I've made a few
        of my own)
love to buy new tools
        hang them along the walls they
        watch me
love to work
        with tools that have keen edges I feel
        the beauty of the edge from deep
        inside
        my hand
I work with only six knives
        each one has a purpose
use a sound-hole knife
        a bridge knife a purfling
        knife a big knife
        for very rough work an all-purpose
        knife I've shaped a table knife
        to open instruments
I've owned these knives
        all my working life I never use
        the new ones
last night while cutting a bridge I dropped
        a knife so sharp
        it stuck in the back of my leg

Two-million-dollar Strad

the trouble
with old fiddles is this
they're old
fiddles open them
up open a hundred violins
by Stradivari you'll see cracks and
worm holes
the bass bars are new the tops are
patched
in the centre new wood there's more
new wood and glue
than old wood

does glue have good
resonant qualities do
worm holes can the glue
and new wood of
Jacobus Crapaud trans-
mogrify
into the wood of Stradivari hocus-
pocus pooh by
sticking to it a peanut
butter sandwich old

fiddles
can never be better
than modern ones two
million dollars! it's
of course
the same with
modern
poems and
poets

Mistakes
November 17, 1982

1. I

2. am a

3. lonely man

4. all my wives have

5. left me they've run off

6. with my apprentices

7. my violins and my wood

8. all my wives one every five years

9. they have taken my children they say

8. they are tired of my complaints I

7. am a lonely man made so

6. many mistakes why is

5. every one out to

4. cheat me even

3. my friends want

2. to cheat

1. me

(Order)

shop thinking of the shop tonight swept dusted vacuumed
washed stacked hung full day's cleaning organizing primp
and preen now feel the glow from my hands up my arms
down into my belly my legs glow thinking of the shop
everything in its own place every tool in its bed on its hook
every piece of wood waxed marked the date when I
received it from whom and where every jar of varnish
tagged named empty box placed ready to catch the shavings
floor bench cleared papers filed moisture in the air
controlled I know the order need to brag to Sara here at
supper could go there in the middle of the night the dark
wouldn't need a light no light no switch what do you want?
tell me the half-inch gouge? the purfling chisel? coping saw?
the driest piece of spruce? wouldn't take a second here it is
see? everything's in order need to keep a semblance of
order pretend there is order pattern harmony so little order
anywhere else in the world today order such an old man

Holy Land

visit
to the
Middle
East stop
at all the
shrines icons
temples wander
in the desert dip
my hand in the
dead
sea lick my finger
taste it drink wine with
two old Hungarian
friends in Tel Aviv
deliver a violin
for the symphony scrape
and bow all those people that
war they lived through
war I lived through death all
around and more fighting now too
much fighting war
lost feeling inside me disjunction
and besides I miss the press
of the chisel in the palm of my hand
long
for the warmth of my block plane
dream the touch of the gouge
and the calliper on my skin ache for
the wind and the cold
Canadian
winter

Arch-aeology 3

                                  the puritans
                  thought the violin
                    a gift from
                                          the arch-

                  fiend
                                      the fallen
        arch
                                              something
                  about the sound
          cat
                      gut and horse
            tail the yowl
                                      and screech

                                      of the violin
                        devil always
          plies
                        a violin

Catgut?

wrong! sheep entrails!

guts sheep viscera small
intestine the alimentary
canal pharaohs
started it along
the Nile so the story goes
pharaohs resting in their easy
chairs eunuchs
fans waving round them minstrels
with their plucked gu(i)tars
workers cutting stone moving
giant stone pyramids
another death
to come another
life strings

for violin
for viol
viola da gamba clean and
scrape and cure don't believe me?
I can show you step by step
instructions those pharaohs
started it the
killing sheep for
gut small intestine also
used for tennis
rackets surgical
ligatures (think I'm
stringing you
a line?)

Tone poem

how do you build
sound the tone of
Stradivari

one small slip of
the gouge a hole
in the d string

You can build a Stradivari

do you love the violin
would you like to build
one the amateur
violinmaker can follow
no better pattern than
a Stradivarius

you can build a
Stradivari provides the
craftsperson with exact
instructions for copying
Antonius Stradivari's
1716 Messiah

in the pocket at the
front of this book you
will discover a set of
eight full-size drawings

anyone with a knack
for woodworking and
a little patience can
utilize these drawings to
produce a fine-toned
violin in the style of the
great Italian masters

Joseph V. Reid
Popular Mechanics Press
Chicago, 1950.................$1.95

Jew or Catholic, Muslim

Basilique Notre Dame in Montreal what a large and powerful
cathedral (maybe not as beautiful as those in old Budapest oh
Budapest) read the pictures in the stained glass sun and figures in
the stained glass twist to stare at the ceiling slide my hand along a
pillar smell the wax the candles love to watch the rows of candles
doors open close again sing-song of the priest echo through the
building new dollar coin from my pocket drop it in the jar light a
candle flame flickers in the wind

not a Catholic not sure what I am a Jew? Buddhist? Atheist?
none of those really all of them light this candle in the Basilique
Notre Dame in Montreal think of my parents mother dead long
ago father dead too candle for my parents Margie smiles and puts
her hand on my arm I hope now they can be together again my
father's dream those last years in Budapest pious man that was all
he wanted soon we will all be together again he told me that

all these candles in the Notre Dame watch the candles hundreds of
candles who lit all these candles so many older women here all
these people all their trouble this is for my husband he works too
hard this for my pregnant daughter bless her find her a good man
for my son who has cancer for my dead mother this is for my wife
who cries and cries for my brother help him to stop drinking

what will happen to the world the world and all its trouble
government carries such a large debt so many people out of work
war and killing everywhere Middle East world swollen with greed
and anger remember the communists and the revolution will there
ever be tanks in Canada someday old man I see death everywhere
I have learned to always think the worst I sit and I watch and my
arms ache so much sorrow

Art of lutherie

prolonged exposure to dust particles from tropical
old world trees genus diospyros dalbergia ebony
rosewood or of the arborvitae evergreen trees of
the cypress family genus thuja plicata western red
cedar inspiration of fibres saw and file dust from
several species of marine shell mother of pearl and
abalone use of commercial abrasives commonly
comprised of aluminum oxide or silicon carbide
sandpaper poison may result in respiratory
ailments bronchial disorders asthma rhinitis and
mucosal irritations in your lungs as well as skin
and eye allergies dermatitis conjunctivitis itching
and rashes improper use of machinery band saws
jointers routers may result in the permanent loss of
appendages fingers bleeding flying projectiles loss
of vision auditory capacity eyes and ears modern
glues often contain cancer-causing agents crazy
glues etc. welcome to the art of lutherie it may
cause long-term or short-term illness and death

Violins and poetry
1995

I am a poor man

I have holes in my pockets
I have a shop full of wood and violins
I have a bag full of memories
I had hopes
I have holes in my pockets
I need to pay the mortgage and the rent

I am a poor man
I am poor as a poet
my heart swells with the ache   the thought of old places
        dead friends
I sit at night and count the total of my losses
is this poverty
I find nothing holy here

I have my honour my honesty
I love my family
love my friends
I care for my violins
I don't believe in the government
        any government
I am a rich man
I have a shop full of empty violins
I have empty pockets

I have a memory of home and Hungary
I love Hungary
love poetry
love laughter and sorrow
love gypsies and tears and violins

I'm a poet praying in my prison
a craftsman tangled in his trade
I have subtracted my worth from my debt
zero is a human number

I wish I could reach the beauty of the sky
wish I could stretch the moon and the stars
      touch the song of that blue bird
      hold the scarlet of the tanager
I wish I could pour them all in my chest
      my empty chest
fill the hole of my missing children
I have holes in my pockets
I am a poor man

there were beggars before the revolution
there are beggars after the revolution
there are beggars here in Canada
I am a beggar
I have nothing left to lose

from *Under the Wings of Africa*
(2007)

Thunderbird 2

Lightning slash
peels me
skin
from skin
dermis
from epi-
dermis from
nerve and
lymph more
naked now
than ever
bound
but exposed
fire
where once
your fingers
touched me
oh
sweet pain
oh sweet
sorrow

(please
sing it again!)

Thunderbird 3

Your skin remembered
the soft round feel of it
and smell the edge
of my nostrils
your lips moist searching
your hair in my face
on my chest
and your fingernails
deep and burrowed in my arms
hard! desire!
your legs astraddle
beginning to quiver
and your cry
now now my cry
she's gone

you said once
this absence would
represent
a test (I say, some cross-
examination or-
deal by fire a holy
catechism-
clysm) but
if I still breathe on my return
if this conflagration
still blazes in my breast
tell me have I won
or have I lost

(and tell me this
how did you earn the right
to judge me?)

Bird Has Flown

Some acrostic floating the currents between us. A question perhaps
you hoped to ask? I don't know. You told me the afternoon we met

you already had a lover, a husband you said. And children. The
first words you spoke. Nearly. You said you liked my hands. Big

hands. You cradled them in yours; you said they looked strong.
You said: Don't expect too much. And I answered: Expect

everything. I said: Be happy when you don't get it. You spoke
again: I already have a lover. Those words repeated. A dark night.

Not a speck of moon. So very dark. I couldn't see the shadows. I
couldn't see the flashlight in my hand, or the trees. Couldn't see

the pines, nor the giant cones, the trail. Couldn't see birds, or hear
them. Couldn't see your finger as it touched my nose, or your lips

as you circled to kiss me. I took a deep breath, your soft body
smell. I realized then that the dandelion lay already twisted in its

bed, that the sun and moon and stars had fallen from the heavens.
The birds had died, and their song with them. I noticed a snap in

the marrow of my bones, a searing in my heart. I tried to speak
again, I thought there must be some thing I could say. I opened my

mouth but no word sounded. Only my aching stumbling tongue.
What does this mean, this lifelong craving, this longing for words?

Bee Bird

I know friendship, its uncomplicated nature, its wealth. I have many friends, good friends; they come to me with ease. But I have found no path through the mystery of love, no solution to its logarithms. Love feels bad, feels good. My love and I, our dance proves difficult. We step together, we drift apart; we love, we hate.

Here on the lee side of a knoll I lie and watch the ibis settle round me. That pair of wagtails calling, or the Egyptian geese, what answers have they found to the cry of their mates, in the flapping of the other's wings.

Somehow, everywhere I go these days my death watches me. I know it's age, mine, my father's. I don't know what it is; these clouds above Paarl never seem to move at all. Whom can I call to, what god, or goddess, to help me clear the mysteries of life.

This tan pup, with the black nose and curled tail, the same one as a month ago, finds me again here in the valley and comes to me. I'm not a dog person, but this is a person dog. He rolls and wriggles for me, he leads me, follows me. When I speak, he listens.

And then a tractor roars down the hill toward me. I spoke to the driver a half hour earlier, an old black man. I said, Hello. The sun, I said, and pointed. Nice day. He shook his head. He didn't understand my language, or I his; he, and his granddaughter beside him.

Now he opens his tractor window again and reaches a bundle of grapes out to me. I take it, and smile, stunned by the grandeur of his gift. The driver waves. The tractor turns and races up the hill again. One moment, then I wake from my stupor. Tell me, I call through the snarl of the tractor; tell me, I cry, what do you know about the miracle of love.

Thunderbird 4

Dark morning
black clouds and the pouring rain
against my skin
rain-soaked clothes and skin
just standing there
under the monkey thorn
with thunder

the stink of lightning
my burning skin,
and crying
my head saying
she's gone!
she packed her bags

she stepped on the bus
she's travelling
or one of those big black clouds

opened and swallowed her
she turned up the sound
and the music took her
gone!
she's gone!

Bird One Stone

broken
latch front door
and bangs the wind
house howling
and when I look

          falling from cloud

             and the sun
               you and I

gathered
morning's orange flowers
on the floor
lie crushed and

        hope might grow

        or pearl I thought
           flower maybe

pillow
the pearl
where I laid it
was gone I thought
maybe this stone
something would grow
and then a garden

       something an orange

              lost
          as though
    and sorrow rushing

like hope
sun breaking
from first to last
cloud

        the front door
         wind howls

from *Where Calling Birds Gather*
(2013)

1.2 Prairie Tale

(relativity)

winter winnipeg   double digit cold thirties frigid forties   and
weier's wearing double layers wool fleece   triple and quadruple

layers   fur eider   hopes to keep the warm in if he dares step
out   otherwise he's thinking sun warm holiday   bird holiday

thinking spur-winged plover   bronze mannikin   black-billed
barbet holiday   thinking africa   thinking suntan   thinking

home and gold-brown mate for the coming spring summer fall
gold-limbed summer winter fall   so he flies to addis ababa

pulls muscle shirt shorts open-toed sandals from his suitcase
struts the street people staring   mad dog englishman   white

canadian cuckoo   notices black ethiopians wear capes shawls
long pants   long-sleeved shirts   sometimes two shirts and

blazers in blazing temps   double digit thirties   fiery forties
only hands faces in ethiopia exposed to sun   as if layers keep

the cool of the body in   as if he knows anything   as if weier
understands anything at all in this cold hot complicated light

1.8 Argument

stand in line
cairns airport
step to the counter

officer: where you from

tourist: canada

officer: what you got

tourist: binoculars

officer: why you in australia

tourist: birdwatcher come to look for birds

officer: oh cassowary   you've come to see cassowary
              it's a magnificent bird   i see the mom every
              spring when she stalks down out of the rainforest
              chicks following   they wander the beach at etty
              bay   my grandma lives there   in etty bay
              let me give you her address and phone number

2.2 Compass

                    sand track
          cattle trail
                    dust
                         bowl or dried
riverbed
                                   not an inch of tarmac
                                   three hundred kilometres

               stone corduroy
                         anthology of boulders
plait of rocks
                    across the water
                                   not my car not yours
                                   acura bmw wouldn't
                                        last an hour

               the slash between forest
on the right
                                   fecund forest
                         on the left
a rash of thorns
                                   consider the laws we live by
                                   consider the lives we live

               these ruts and cuts
zagging
                         the sun-glazed hill
                              so one day heaves into another
this course between chestnut-naped
                    and crested francolin
          at last
                         all these synonyms for road

2.3 Tablature

soil
african
soil red-brown
       soil the way it ripples
       drifts the way it spins
       swirls devils

in circles yowls
whorls the way
it straddles
       the wind and sand
       sand sun
       swept sand

its heat its fervour
its reek
of dark solitude
       the hourglass
       way it tickles past
       his fingers

and chanting
goshawk the way
it slides
       through his thirsty
       hands (six
       psalms to go)

2.5 Definition

flightless bird native
                    to queensland   tall
            as a tall person two
            metres and ostrich-shaped
black plumage
            bright blue
                        neck red wattles
            according to pictures
                        brown casque on head
eats fruit
                        fallen or hanging
            from low branches
                        sometimes frogs
            snails snakes insects

casuarius casuarius
southern cassowary female
            bigger more vivid
                            than male
lays three eggs
                    on rainforest
            floor   only the male
incubates   only
                        the male cares
for chicks   nine
                        months' care
while female wanders
                        seeks out
            another mate   no cockerel/
                    husband complaints
clamouring
                        in her handbag
            or twice as many

99

3.2 Prairie Tale

riding the back roads of australia
        chasing sun rain mud   running
        down wind dust flood   chasing forest
mountain marsh   passing cars   trucks
        being passed when he stops
        at the bend to goggle some post-perched
        bird   some pied and spectacled monarch

his children's lives   though now
        they're grown he could surely stop
        calling them children   but what to call
        them instead   issue or offspring
progeny   his son and daughter
        their lives   what fills their days   today

this sun rainy day   what fragment
        of jubilant song   what far-flung
        wound   humdrum of dishes
or laundry or paint   do they laugh
        at their work   do their bosses speak
        kind words or cruel   do their lovers
love them in fact or hover and skulk
        like butcherbirds   will they have children
will they be better parents than he   knows
        he could have done
                wishes he had

but wishes or horses or beggars   and given
            the nature of time   this circle of blue
            green earth   rainbow of birth life
            death   maybe it's night for them
asleep   he remembers their child
            faces   how once he leaned
            over them in their slumber
here on the side roads of australia
            his children's lives   love
            and those cradle days   wonders
what are they dreaming today

3.6 Argument

weier stops to buy
          groceries for the road
          store full of shoppers

let's see
          nuts cheese apples
          carrots
          bananas granola
          toothpaste   one big
          shopping basket

grocer: why did cassowary cross the road
shopper: see if he could get run over by a car

grocer: why did cassowary cross the road
shopper: because sign said cassowary crossing

grocer: why did cassowary cross the road
shopper: see if she could find a tourist

          and everybody laughs

weier's confused embarrassed
          are they laughing at him
          should he check
          his fly   would anyone notice

3.8 Definition

what is it his body
    brain being needs
        right
    now
at twelve fourteen
    on a monday afternoon
while songbirds fidget
    and fret
    in the shrubbery

      while frogmouth
sleeps and cathedral fig
    ficus virens weaves
      its sinister
nest   while wind
    pushes pulls clouds
    scud   australian sun
lingers above these arms
    legs ribs these fingers
    toes   what are they
      begging for

this heart this heaving
    blood these animal
    bones   what's
their question

5.2 Crossing

next day
he fights

back   bites
back   turns

to the window
calls species
names in defiance
calls
mountain thrush
cape canary

common bulbul   pulls
out imaginary
tape measure   magic
marker   marks

his space   see
this line   pushes out
hips elbows shoulders
owns his full third
of back seat   see

the black line he shouts
augur buzzard
red-faced crombec
purple grenadier
shrieks
bateleur

don't cross it

5.5 Prairie Tale

long hours behind the wheel   dust   sun   heat   driving
hills flats   driving desert revving roads   ridged rutted

fluted furrowed roads   roads guttered by last year's rain
eyes straight ahead sileshi drives   short   slight   dark

curly haired   smiling always smiling sileshi slows speeds
weaves   sileshi avoids holes craters disaster   dodges a

montagu's harrier at dusk   but in the worlds before and
after driving while we search for birds he parks his toyota

under the camel thorn   acacia   if he finds one   wanders
a pocket-sized perimeter of shade   i watch him through

binoculars a half kilometre away   voyeur   watch his
mouth   lips   hands   movement   he's singing   perhaps

the jazz tones of the woman tsedenia   (do i hear drum
boom in the distance)   or he's practising English   yes

english phrasebook in hand   all sileshi's languages   later
after black-crowned tchagra and lichtenstein's sandgrouse

when we get back from our search he pulls a thorn from
the camel tree asks what the word is   how do you write

he says   i spell   t h o r n   and holding the thorn like
a pencil he scratches the letters in white on his forearm

5.10 Songlines

sends an email to a friend   tells her here in australia
he's lonely   she emails back   reminds him he's
lonely in winnipeg too   how can this be
                                        he has two

children who love him   twelve siblings   nine
hundred twenty-seven names in his address book
                        if he used abacus
        maybe they'd all
                                add up
                                        help him

feel rounded
                more grounded
                                less
of a plains wanderer
        (the word abacus as first recorded in middle
english in 1387 derived from the hebrew for dust)

7.3 Definition

cassowary's a good
        runner they say
        wikipedia says   fifty
kilometres per hour
        through tropical
        rainforest   good jumper
two metres high
        over its own two-metre
        cassowary mate   excellent
swimmer and fighter too
              six razor
        claws   can disembowel

an enemy   kill
        with one blow
        and will in defence
        of nest and young
for which we
        judge it
            violent
                vicious

the most dangerous
        bird in the world

9.3 Tablature

sacred ibis
           sways
        at the tip
     of a spindle
juniper   abyssinian
           white-eye
       flutters in the spray
    from a leaky green
garden hose   little
            rock-thrush and
        streaky seedeater
    skulk deep
in the undergrowth

brown-rumped serin
       scratch
   scratch
scratches at the dust
         (eighty-five
     psalms)
the way it mimics
        the un-
           common
house sparrow

10.2 Crossing

what would his kids say if they knew he was out here
in nowhere australia wandering a long dirt road in the
wasteland   he and the nine most toxic arachnids on the
planet   what would they say if they knew he was walking
a rainforest trail   hadn't seen woman man dog cat mouse

since quitting the highway four hours back   should he
fall   break an ankle   crack head on a boulder feel chest
pain   should anything happen he'd be lucky some park
ranger would notice his car in the parking lot two days in a
row and come looking   what would his daughter son say

if they understood how much he's been bitten up sweating
australian wetlands   hunting black bittern and rufous-
tailed bush-hen   hunting something to write   arms legs
lumped pitted pocked bloodstain scabbed   armies of bugs
his body their no-man's land   if they saw how his heart

thumps nights he looks in the mirror sees the face of the
boy   some days his heart rolls round and around in his
chest inside an empty drum   and his heart feels what it
feels allows nothing else   if they knew the last woman he
loved shared their age breaking the rule   if he told them

his friends had somehow grown old   had forgotten   had
left him to flounder   what would they say if they heard
wednesday above stoney creek falls he found cuckoo-shrike
high on a wire catching flies   common cicadabird singing
from high in a telephone wire   and what would they say

10.4 Stone-Broke

hank williams says lonesome whippoorwill
dolly parton says loneliness found me one time too many
elvis says been so long on lonely street
    and billie holiday travelling alone
joni mitchell says am a lonely painter in a box of paints
beatles say sergeant pepper's lonely hearts club

text says loneliness a symptom of depression
    free online dictionary strong feeling of emptiness isolation
king james says i am desolate and afflicted
    says nothing about loneliness at all
    though concordance squeezes it between
                loins and longing

ironically people are often loneliest in areas of heavy population
    seem to have been particularly lonely this past century
    wikipedia says

that shakespeare was one of the first
        writers to record the world
    like to a lonely dragon that his fen makes feared
buddhist pema chodron says
    born alone   die alone   in between also alone
    loneliness at heart of being human

dalai lama says cultivate compassion
teilhard de chardin says world round like a ball
    friendship round too
torresian crow says caw caw caw
    and shuffles its wings

11.6 Songlines

imagine

                        what it means

         to stand all day

                while goats graze

                and blackcap calls above

       a windburnt sun

                acacia twig for shade

imagine

11.7 Prairie Tale

in the loo at the airport in addis ababa   weier sits listens as two
twenties boy men bluster above their urinals   they take their time
talking as young men do   about women about beer   not playful

at all but still wordplay   and running a score   near young man
eight   far young man zero   i called home the near one shouts
and my mom said we had three feet snow last night   seconds

of silence   gush of tap water   slur of paper towel rolled from
dispenser   that's nothing he says compared to five feet we had in
january eight years ago   cock-of-the-block he is   or helmeted

guineafowl   all his bigger better numbers   (measure perhaps for
pygmy falcon)   silence again   then rustle of toothbrush   more
water more towel   sound of footsteps   sounds of leaving and

the second one voice fading around the corner   huh he says (two
can play this game)   we had fifteen feet snow
                                    in one day he says
          last year at my house he says
                    in the middle of august

must be a bad week weier thinks where he rests on his porcelain
throne   tough week for those two if all they can boast about here
in addis ababa is storm and winter weather   could be two prairie

old-timers weier thinks   chuckles   (sure he's the old-timer eaves-
dropping)   and canadians probably   one from edmonton   one
yellowknife   telling tall tales about weather   tall tales about home

their talk about home   while he sits on the loo here in addis
ababa (fidel castro madonna the pope queen all do it)   scribbles
the words

        in his notebook

home

                he writes
that's home for you

12.3 Argument

(letter to the editor)

i personally despite serious endeavour have not
observed any living cassowary in all my thirty days
sojourn in queensland   nor have i encountered one
visitor from foreign shores in similar pursuit more
fortunate than i   this strikes me as implausible given
said creatures' profile both in the common travel
literature and in local repartee   i have come finally
and sorrowfully to conclude that cassowary does not
in fact exist   i believe cassowary to be an illusion
(barn owl and honey fungus ignis fatuus) created by
a covetous collection of governments anxious to lure
unsuspecting foreigners to provincial resort town
and villages   to places like etty bay mission beach
daydream beach dunk island   where they may be
more successfully preyed upon   an elaborate system
of road signs and billboards has been constructed to
support this cassowary delusion and local officials
have gone to the extreme of hiring students to plant
scatterings of so-called cassowary dung on the
periphery of rainforest trails   scatterings that i have
scrutinized and now judge to be more credible as
processed pony turd   i write this note to remind
tourist boards and travel agents that we foreigners
we canadians at least   are not so easily stripped of
our hard-earned savings   we are not so easily duped

12.4 Tablature

earth
>> blue green
>> planet   our home
the loss of it
>> loss of all this
and love flown
>> hourglass sand
>> snow sting sand
>> ethiopian sand falling

the death that follows
>> death of things
>> my death
>> yours   one hundred
>> twenty-seven
>> psalms   a burning wind
and our lives
>> irretrievable irresistible
>> angels
the language of angels
>> their breath
>> the rush of wings

all these wonders
>> and lives irrepressible
whisper
>> of angel wings
>> and little
>> ringed plover

New Poems
Refuge

1.1 first flight

cool misty morning in August
      an hour past sunrise and you're
onto the bike   old Rockhopper
      three decades-old hands
handlebars pedals and balls

      of your feet and you pedal on down
the block   take a long left turn
      and you're out on the river road
wind at your back   now push
      you say   push hard   push man

push that crank push   teach
      those knubby mountain tires
how to sing   shift gears   suck
      air   watch road-cracks skip by
watch two brown legs pump

      pump   pump like you're six
or eleven   pump like you're
      finally seventy-two   the training
you cannot forget   the feeling
      accelerate exhilarate   this body

old body   this one body   one
      life   joy of the body   push hard
push push   push man   lift your arms
      and sail on   fly strong man   fly
old man   come fly with the wind

1.2 cradle song

you've been tracking the black-backed woodpecker you heard
                    tap tap tap
from the side of the snow road   you been bushwhacking
                scratching scraping scouring through thicket black spruce
white birch balsam fir aspen and tamarack   squeezing straggling
                        staggering into up over and under saskatoon
dogwood and hawthorn   through deadfall
                                                through downfall
where branches that snap under knee-deep snow keep you
                        jilting jeetering jottering
just on the edge of balance you're unbalanced when suddenly

you lurch into a hollow   slight dent in the ground like a bowl
                    or maybe a human-sized basket   a sort of clearing
in the deep dank dark forest   a circle   and what
                                and you stop   stop
the crash and the clatter   stop the chase   you settle
            on the bole of a fallen spruce and notice you're gasping
                            heart's racing   notice
that something's coming up coming down   a feeling
                                of homecoming
            though the wintry wind still rages in the treetops above
just like that   you settle   and your breath

slows heart eases muscles begin to loosen   and a chickadee lights
            in the buckthorn beside you   looks at you
then for a moment   for one moment you think that one thought
            about the future   dying thought and not at all sorrowful
                    it turns out   then the chickadee flits
        to your shoulder   feathers on your shoulder

and the woodpecker flies into view not five metres distant
            black back black crown   beak that tap tap taps
                    at the bark of a pine where you sit   where you watch
from the circle   stopped here in the circle   where you cradle
                                in the great circle of time

2.1 automatic

wears tactical vest   coyote
      brown by Condor catalogue
    matching pants   pair of high-top
hiking boots   long and raven hair
            like from a song
       and drawn back
into ponytail   black brows   black
      jacket under vest   dressed

        to kill   carries gun as proof
   looks confident comfortable
         holding Kalashnikov
  or Romanian AK-47 acute-
        angled across her chest
one hand on stock   other hand
    on magazine   and you know nothing
      about guns   what you read

yesterday on Wikipedia   but recognize
       wooden stock and grip and hand
     guard golden grain of cherry
wood   hand-polished
   lustre   and you don't know
      cannot imagine
     anything about actual enemies
        about Czech hedgehog

barriers to her right   the couple
rolls barbed wire bristling
on the left   blue road sign pointing
behind   and you ask yourself
isn't she scared   doesn't
look it   no fear the picture
reveals   more intent determined
and you wonder

what's she thinking as she stares
north along road
your distant cousin maybe
or niece three times
removed   what's she thinking
as she watches north
along highway
with road sign behind in bold
letters naming her birth
place   naming bombed-out
home   Welcome
Mariupol

2.2 line-dancing

you grind beans and set the coffee brewing
    pour a glass of juice and sip till the timer dings
quiche ready to pop from the oven   smells
    good   when suddenly
          there she is on tv   speaking

to the BBC from Kherson in Ukraine   yes she says
    we have flour   bake our own bread
         get potatoes from the farm
but most of what we eat she says we have to stand
    in line   a pound of meat a couple

eggs   yesterday I waited two hours to buy milk
       while Mam took care of the girls
you see the girls now on tv   blonde heads bobbing
    at the bottom of the screen   eyes reaching
for you over the table's

edge   just that much too short for the camera
they miss their dad she says pats one on the head
       yesterday was cold she says
by the time it was my turn the milk was gone
          you see her eyes move

to the corner of the room   see her lips tremble
   see tears she's crying   such struggle such sorrow
such fear   and you notice your own tears   a welling
   in your chest   her name's Nadiya
       you mean to remember that   but already

the news clip's ended and Nadiya's gone   her daughters
gone   war-torn Ukraine gone   tv's moved on
                          to credit scores mouthwash best
shampoo or moisturizer greener grass better burgers
            you sigh and reach for the oven mitt

                        reach for the quiche   grab
        a knife and fork   yum   already
you've forgotten

2.3 stone's throw

dressed in jeans and parka   wisp
                    of blonde hair slipped
from under the toque   and Blundstones
            on her feet like any cool Canadian   she's
                        waiting   bulging knapsack
                            draped across her back   baby

on her arm six-month-old
                cradled in arm   sitting   waiting
        but where's she going   who's she with
            who's waiting with her for her   the train
                    she says to Dnipro
                she says to Kiev Lviv to Krakow   mother's

found a room in Krakow   if every thing
                        goes she says   if
    every thing is okay she says still takes a long
                time and what then
                    I'd rather go home she says to Mariupol
        but she's seen pictures and there's nothing

left nothing   her husband stayed in Mariupol he
                has a gun   he stayed I left she says
                        he's fighting but he sent
            pictures   I'd rather go home   but where's
                home   there's nothing
                        but rubble she says   no one left

she says a train   two thousand kilometres
                mother has a room she says   she
        and these hundred thousand
                    others   they're hoping
                                for a train

1.3 snow blind

far-flung and brazen
                prairie after a lengthy
        bone-deep snowfall
it's into the minus thirties today
                wind and snow sweeping
        across fields   straddling
            roads   skittering
                        through ditches
and probably you shouldn't

            be out in these crazy temps
but you are   you're fit enough
    and dressed for winter
                    it wouldn't hurt
        if you had to walk a mile
or two   the car's repaired
        and well-equipped to travel
dirt and gravel backroads   these almost
        prairie roads   and you can't resist

                the faint haze of woodlot in the distance
                    the farmhouse snuggled
                in its sheltered rows of trees
                        caducous and conifer
            the snowy lump of feathers hunkered
                on the fifth post of pasture
                    there in the east-west line
                        owl on an ivy bush
            cannot resist the centuries

of tallgrass waving and dreaming
                         or the thought of Bob
who used to come this way
              on blustery afternoons
                         and who could refuse
        the cold and wind and snow
the open space
              who could resist this home
                   this wild and joyful home

1.4 cross your heart

but where do you find
            hope she says suddenly
    breaking the flow   and maybe
                it's age that makes
        the answer today
so much easier   or maybe
                    he's distracted
        by the glint of sun
                in the window
                    behind her

                    by the memory
                of goldenrod blooming
        beside the trail   the chorus
                        of last night's rain
            by the morning scent of rose
                        mallow and meadow
        blazingstar   the moon and the fresh
                    tomato   the silence
            of mixed forest   the soft
            and soughing wind   distracted

by the group of them
            sitting in a cluster
        with their books
and their youth   by conversation
                interrelation   by laughter
by the sorrow and need
                that shine in her eye because
        that's where he finds it   hope
        and what's hope anyway
                tentative   temporary
        hesitant as mercy   tender
as a bruise

3.1 drops names

hardwoods
epená   carapa   cramantee
árbol de Santa Maria
and fruiting palms   pambil
and yanchi   trees tower
above the shadowed trails of tandayapa
west slope Andes   cloud forest trees   drink
from leaves instead of roots   grow five
metres each year   hundred species trees
in one small square kilometre   high
canopy   u   middle canopy
n
d
e
r
s
t
o
r
y   forest home
to puma kinkajou spectacled bear and little big-eared bat   to
hundreds species of hawk moth lappet moth tiger moth   and hundred more
species butterfly peacock tortoiseshell brown   home to great flocks
of tanagers   a tango   a tangle a tassel
a tussle a tantrum or tempest
torment   torture
tarnation   and tabulation
tribulation of tanagers
eighty tanager species possible this one rainforest
and how will she ever name them
keep them straight
it's impossible

3.2 cryptogram

thumping
    stumping
        galumphing along
            the rocky road
      rough and rugged
           mud and rutted
never dusty road
           with Yanacocha rain
                clouds both
           below above
        this hanging on the edge
             of mountain

        acrophobic road
hump and pound road
     bump and bound
   crash smash
      shake and shatter road   hands
          are trembling knees
           feel weak   pen leaps

        up down all around road
             and wonder
     you wonder who
        in the dark days ahead
     will decipher
   this squiggled page of code
story of a two-track
      knife edge
        of the mountain
    this humming-
      bird and condor sanctum
high in the Andes road

1.5 incantation

and what if she sat by the window and padded the words tropical
forest onto the keyboard
       yesteryear's northern winter
   when she walked on the trails above Ubatuba
        over hills along valleys
through sun and mist and rain eyes ears nose skin all prickling

awakening what if she set that on this make-believe paper
        what if she called to the trees
    named them rosewood laurel
papaya mangrove and candelabra pine
           cedar and pau brasil
or summoned the undergrowth maranta heliconia calliandra

   philodendron and bromeliad
      orchid and saprophyte long
leaf short leaf round leaf and pointed oblong serrated
denticulated leaves their countless
        colours green their
lush and lofty luxuriance their radiant blossoms red orange

yellowblue indigo and violet what if she spoke these words
shouted them if she set her belief in them would they come
      to her call would trees spill
   from the monitor rich and robust
vigorous vivacious trees teeming
        tumescent would leaves

shatter the window glass would beams above sprout branches
   and boughs would violence
        and voracity would life flowering
fertile fecund fructiferous life vulgar and visceral erupt
   on the desk in her studio would howler monkeys
       gather to bellow and bawl

from the chandeliers   would coatis snuffle and grunt
in the laundry   and white-bearded manakins
                                  fly room to room
binging on berries in bookshelves
                       would diademed tanagers forage
for flies in the fallen and fetid debris on yesterday's vacuumed

and polished floors
                   and after a glass of wine   a sampling
of bread cheese and broccoli   would the sound of insects
      so loud in the thicket sing her to sleep
in her bed even here in the frozen Canadian tundra
         would insects sing even here
               in this distant and frozen tundra

1.6 small fortune

rain and rain and rain
        two days rain   morning rain
     evening rain   rain pounding
on roof   rain rumbling
              on roof   rain pelting
      the window glass
                  gurgling
the eaves   rain rain and rain

                thunder lightning
         and beating rain backyard
      turn into a lake
          back alley a river

         sidewalk under
water gazebo threatens
      to float   rain rain more rain
    come rushing down crashing
        down crushing down but
this little house
      this hundred-year

        house no pails on the throw
    rugs or pans on the hardwood
           floor no water drip
     from the ceiling no puddles
   in basement this house

                    this haven home
refuge house
            keeps me warm dry
                    keeps me sheltered
so lucky me   and I mean it
                            so bloody
            lucky me

1.7 winter pronoun

Winnipeg morning dark as dark city can be   ice on road
snow piled on curb cold car grumble groan every stop
                and dashboard display

                                minus 25 brrr

                                        plus north

wind and windchill for sure   buildings
all round send chimney smoke scudding
                straight and narrow
                straight man straight
                        from a horse's mouth

                                        south

                you think coffee
cold crack of dawn it's coffee
you want and you pull into a drive
thru you order pull up

                                        and behold
                        and behoof there's a bike
                        at the window ahead of you
                                fat tire bike

and a rider too all bungled in parka
snowpants and boots Michelin
manikin lookalike

                                and they reach
                        with their gloved hand to grab
                        coffee a paper bag muffin
                        maybe or breakfast
                                        sandwich
                and quickly they're up on their pedals they're
gone while you in your car just now starting to warm
snuggle your heated seat   thanking the happy go lucky
stars you're that much too old for bikes

                                and raw winter riding

2.4 flight risk

1.

night comes
                  dark
     not even moon
     not even whisper of wind
           after day's heat

and wakes the children
     four girls six to thirteen
              a kiss
     finger across their lips
            no talking
wakes the old one
     grandmother   hours before

          the muezzin
      that nobody knows
not children
not neighbours
        packed their bags
     and hidden in the shed

hang from shoulder bags
     small for youngest
     medium for oldest
       a few pieces clothing
     hard bread and cheese
     dried strips goat meat

bag full of fear
   she shoulders
      full of certainty courage
     prayer full of
life death uncertainty
     and life again here
and gone here
        and gone

2.

Kabul to Karachi bearings
    scrawled on scrap
       they walk sweat
squat on riverbank
    spill water over heads
       pass through throat
of canyon throat
    of thirst hunger throat
       scramble over under
rocks round boulders
    they climb cross mountain
       pass where Flanders
poppies blooming blow
    five days nights desert
      sand and her girls
are strong girls patient
    surprise and surrender
      this Afghan birthright
and succour sometimes
    one donkey cart ride
      two villages supper
six more days nights
   walking and then and then
      scratch line in sand

mark Pakistan border

                they board the train
        money she begged
borrowed   without shame
              and hid in her burqa
       hidden in folds of burqa
starting price   or face value
           she thought was paradise
      somewhere to go   but where
do you go from here

2.5 and mis-fortune

and water
colour of soil water
cascade of mud water
pour through villages water

roar down city streets water
push over bridges   rush round
front doors of houses   rumble
bumble tumble water

                              and countryside water
                      here handmade
                      brick wall three metres by one
                              and ocean of water
                      there five green trees shining
                                          poking heads
                      above water and lone camel
                survivor of desert stands on single
                              promontory of land water
kingdom of water   fish
in meadow   frogs
in pasture water   ducks
on cropland   and water

frogs and turtles water
          cows calves belly-deep water
                up to your waist
                          waste water
      five years rain in three days
where are the roads water
                      climate
                              crisis water   one third Pakistan
under water   one million homes damaged destroyed   bringer
of death water   and still more water

3.3 storm blown

night and day south out of Port Stanley the ocean began to swell
and the sky turned from blue to grim and ominous gray   and with
a west wind howling and waves crashing over the bow of the ship

finding every possible opening in our raingear and threatening to
snatch our bins and cameras and spotting scopes   threatening to
throw us over and against the rail and the five of us in the counting

crew were enjoined to move indoors and off the promenade   few
birds to record in this weather anyway and we went willingly but
watched as the doors were bolted and barricaded behind us   and

after stopping by our rooms in the belly of the ship for dry clothes
we made our way along the hall and up four sets of stairs into the
dining room where we gathered our food and settled behind a bank

of sturdy windows to take stock as the storm roared and raged all
around   and it was a storm   hurricane winds and water a wretched
and swirling blackish blue and fifteen metre waves rising the length

of the vessel and pounding against the bulkheads sending spray
heavy against our windows and up into the void above   and still no
one spoke of the repute of this Southern Ocean for treachery no one

spoke the word danger   it was a difficult night that followed and in
my cabin I struggled to sleep struggled to contain my supper   for
no matter which way I tossed or turned I felt the room reeling about

me felt the thunder of each swell as it pushed directly on the other
side of the wall at my elbow   hours went by with the gale pounding
the ship rolling the hopeless chug chug of the engine and in the daze

of sleeplessness seasickness I thought that my life would surely end
that this night in these waters would be my last   until finally I pulled
on my clothes and stumbling to a stair that hadn't been barricaded

I crawled up onto the promenade to see if I could find the horizon
I needed to see the horizon   and wasn't that a relief to find it there
in the distance   to find the seas somewhat subdued and the wind

no longer deafening   and after a time feeling steadier and suddenly
careful to avoid the ship's watch I snuck back to my room and after
arranging the bedding I lay down and soon fell contentedly asleep

3.4 sea lions gambol

and waking mid-morning to stone silence rush up stairs and onto
promenade to find ship stopped along Antarctic shores   find
                                    southern sea smooth
                        as smooth as window
                                        glass and brilliant
blue sky   sun
and glacier's glare
against towering black
                    rock
face the back
                    drop
                        and here
                                    one hundred metres distant
orcas ten eleven
blow and breach and break
                    the sea
surface   while Adelie
                        and macaroni penguins
                    float by on lumps and slabs
            and chunks of ice   or burst like
                        pop
                                    corn from ocean
one brown skua
            sails astern

                            playground for petrels and prions
                                seals and sea lions
                        for black-browed albatross
                                    not to mention
                            krill   krill   this saltwater
sanctuary   pelagic
            paradise   humpback
                        heaven
                            amen

Afterword

A horse, a Bible, and a woman; or reflections on the fall; or from being Mennonite to becoming writer

The Carol Shields Distinguished Lecture, delivered at University of Winnipeg on 12 March 2008, revised in 2024

John Weier

I've worried a lot over the past few months, since I first learned of my responsibilities regarding this event, this *distinguished lecture* event, about the actual meaning of the word lecture. I will tell you; I have a troubled relationship with the word, and it goes back a long way. Almost to the beginning of time, back before I turned six for sure. I was the youngest in a large family of overseers and I grew up getting lectures, not giving them. And yet, here I stand today.

My father used to lecture when I was a boy. That's what I told my friends, *my dad gave me a lecture.* And that was sometimes before, sometimes after the strap. Sometimes both. I had run off with Luke on a bright Sunday afternoon to collect empty pop bottles from the ditches along Creek Road. To exchange them for a chocolate bar at the Wiebe's corner store a mile down the road from my house. In contravention of the fourth commandment: *Thou shalt not work on Sunday.* It hadn't occurred to me yet that the gathering of pop bottles would be considered work, though that changed in a hurry. My father lectured. Delivered his considerable opinion of my misdeeds and shortcomings, of my disobedient and fallen nature. If I continued on my current path, he said, I faced a bleak and miserable future.

I should explain. In those days, in the 1950s, when you brought an empty bottle to the corner store you collected a two-cent refund. The bottles would be dropped back in their wooden crates and sent to the factory and refilled with Pepsi or Orange Crush. And sold again. Yes, refilled a second, a third, a fourth time, they were recycled before recycling was even invented. And with *five* empty pop bottles, you could trade for a ten-cent Coffee Crisp or Snickers chocolate bar. Oh? You wonder about the commandment part of this? Anything to do with trade and purchase on a Sunday afternoon counted as manual labour.

You might think that collecting pop bottles and exchanging them for chocolates on a Sunday afternoon in Southern Ontario is not that serious a crime. But I can assure you it is. Especially if you get caught. And you probably doubt my mathematics. I hear you questioning: How could he possibly remember those two and ten-cent figures after sixty years of trouble, of sweat and hard work? Let me explain it to you. Those two and ten-cent numbers were impressed on my back end in a way that will help me remember much longer than my advanced years. And I still love chocolate far more than is good for me, keeping bars hidden in the freezer to sneak at most inopportune moments. My ignorance of the commandments. They say that ignorance is bliss, but I can tell you it's not true. In my experience ignorance is blisters.

My father lectured when he found out I'd gone on a date with Jacquie, in contravention of the eleventh commandment. My Mennonite ancestors had long ago written up an additional commandment to cover the host of sins not mentioned by the original ten. And most of those sins, it seems to me now, had to do with love and sexuality, with drinking and dancing. *Thou shalt not drink, dance, love, touch, and all things related.* I've grown a bit foggy on the rest of the commandments, but I remember this one well enough.

Yes, I did go on a date with Jacquie. Several dates actually. Well, a long year's worth of dates. I kept it secret as long as I could. I went to a movie with Jacquie, and someone saw us. Dating and movies both mentioned somewhere at the back end of the eleventh. We danced at Jacquie's on Saturday nights, to the music of the Everly Brothers, Bobby Vinton, Jan and Dean. And sometimes Harvey snuck in a half-mickey of rum for us to sample. The eleventh commandment again and again. I don't know who squealed on me, but my father found out.

What Jacqui and I did was innocent enough. We kissed. Long, lingering kisses. Gentle, probing kisses. We kissed and we touched. Oh, Jacquie. And in my innocence, at age seventeen, I never imagined anything more than kissing with Jacquie. Nor wanted more. You say you don't believe me, but it's true. My father didn't believe me either. And in the few days since he'd found out about the movie, he'd imagined much more than kissing. Jacquie's older sister and her boyfriend had imagined more than kissing too and that was the problem. They'd imagined a baby into their arms, and they weren't even married. I'm not sure, at that age, whether I had a clear understanding of what all this meant, this imagining babies. It was a quick lecture, my father's, just a few sentences, and didn't offer much information. But it was distinguished, and I had no trouble understanding, no difficulty catching the meaning of his words. *Thou shalt not see Jacquie anymore!* And there it was, my first relational failure.

My new partner lectures too, over korma and paneer at the East India Company restaurant. I say partner, it's our third date and she's trying to impress me with Jon Kabat-Zinn and his mindfulness practices. I'm trying to impress her with what a good listener I am. This kind of thing, you see, still happens early in relationships, even at my great age—relationships don't necessarily change or get easier with age. This new partner believes in the need for a more balanced and interconnected approach to all the elements of our lives. An integral and mindful approach. And incidentally, to all the elements of our relationship. I listen attentively, try to, I believe in listening. But I have a growing sense that this lecture threatens my already faltering sense of self. When you grow up with six older siblings on one hand and a commanding father on the other, you often feel your self to be under siege.

My long history with lectures! But though I'm a father, it's somehow come about that my children are far more likely to lecture me than the other way around. By which you can gather that I haven't been a proper Dad at all, apart from the problem with commandments, that other major shortcoming. You can call it my life's purpose then, not to lecture. Lectures leave me getting defensive. And soon enough angry, not feelings I want to leave with the people around me. I'd like to be a good listener and learn from what people tell me. But I'm not, and I don't. I can't seem to pay the necessary attention. I *have* attended a few *good* lectures in my life. Here at the University of Winnipeg. But until today the task of delivering one, a lecture, has somehow eluded me.

I've never in my life imagined what it might mean to talk for an hour, I don't know if I can physically do it, if my voice will hold to the challenge. I should warn you as well, that I wasn't able to settle easily on a topic for tonight's discussion. So instead of writing one lecture for you, I've written twenty-four. Maybe we'll have time for all of them, and maybe not. And, in case you're getting nervous, I assure you there'll be no scolding, chastening or commanding in today's lectures. You can relax. I'll call this first one, the lecture I just read to you, let's see, I think I'll call it, *Genesis*. It's a beginning.

Robert Kroetsch, in his celebrated *Seed Catalogue*, writes:

How do you grow a poet?

> For appetite: cod-liver
> oil.
> For bronchitis: mustard
> plasters.
> For pallor and failure to fill
> the woodbox: sulphur
> & molasses.
> For self-abuse: ten Our
> Fathers & ten Hail Marys.
> For regular bowels: Sunny Boy
> Cereal.

The next lecture then, the second, I'll call *Exodus*. Foretelling a probable departure.

148

Several months ago, as part of a course I was taking at the University of Winnipeg, I was asked to bring to class a symbol of my culture of origin. To prepare to talk about that symbol for five or ten minutes. *Issues of Diversity*, that was the name of the course. Our instructor was trying to impress on us that we all, despite the kind of monism that our dominant North American culture encourages, that we all carry with us our cultures of origin. Whether they be Ethiopian or Japanese, whether Anglo-Saxon or Mennonite, whether of wealth or of poverty, whether so-called professional or labour cultures, university educated or not university educated. She was trying to impress on us just how much we bring to our everyday lives long-held assumptions that influence our work, our conversation, our relationships. That many of these assumptions, often the ones we think least about, derive from our culture of origin. To impress on us just how much without thinking we continue to live by our cultures of origin. And coincidentally how these cultures of origin often delineate power differentials. Between men and women. Between races. Between rich and poor. Between parent and child, the parent holding the strap and the child with a blistered bottom. I gained a new understanding in that class for the impact of power differentials in our lives.

But back to the assignment. A symbol of my culture of origin. I remember thinking, in the few moments of silence after the assignment was announced, as we classmates began to digest the task. I remember thinking, what in the world will I ever bring to class as a symbol? I thought of violins, my source of income. I thought of birds or books, my joy. I thought of one of the paintings that hang on my walls at home. I thought of my two grown children. All *symbols* of meaningful parts of my life, but none had anything to do with my origins. And then I thought about books again and before I'd thought for even a second longer about possibilities, I already knew that I'd choose an old falling-apart book that I'd inherited some years ago when my parents died, I'd bring to class the old German family Bible. This Bible, a symbol of my culture of origin. I felt in that moment as though I'd been struck by lightning.

An ancient book, this Bible. Published in Estonia in 1896. After the German translation by Martin Luther. Given to my parents as a wedding gift in 1931. With brown and brittle pages. With a damaged binding, and poorly repaired. With a list of my parents' eight children inscribed on one of the back pages. With birth dates, baptismal dates, marriage dates. And the date of one death, that of my oldest sister, Susie. *Gestorben in Lena Manitoba am 62. Mai 26 1934. Died in the Dirty Thirties.* What causes two-year-olds to suddenly die? I'm guessing a shortage of food and abundance of dust.

The family Bible. I grew up in a very Mennonite home, a religious home. My family went to church every week, often more than once a week. A large red brick church. With square towers. Heavy. Well-defined. Looked more like a fortress than a spiritual haven. I have wondered what we worshipped there. How do you grow a poet? We went to church. We prayed at mealtimes. We had devotions as a family most evenings. Where someone, usually my father from his place at the head of the table, read from the Bible. We children attended a private Christian high school. We believed our Bible to be a sacred text, or we tried to believe, or some of us believed. It was the core symbol of the kind of family we were. Our lives, and our behaviour, judged by a Mennonite understanding of the Bible. My life, and my behaviour, judged. And often found wanting, I might add. Ignorance, you remember, is not bliss at all.

The lecture called *Ruth*, about service and kindness.

When we still had our old barn in Niagara, and before we bought the red Farmall A tractor in 1954, we did all the heavy farm work with our one horse. Molly had a brown coat, and a black mane and tail, a white blaze and long white hair around her hooves. Molly taught me to love the smell of horses. Molly taught me to love the touch and shudder of her skin.

We hitched Molly to the cultivator, a small one, maybe six or seven tines. A shiny and green cultivator. With two handles that my dad could hold as he walked behind. And we, my dad and I and Molly, cultivated between the rows of asparagus. Molly pulled, and my dad followed with the leather reins around his shoulders, hands pushing down on the cultivator. I sat on Molly's back; I enjoyed riding on Molly's back. I held onto the black collar, or onto her mane. I felt Molly's muscles and joints against my bottom. I got a sore bottom. My legs got sore from spreading wide. I felt Molly's sweat against my bum. My pants soaked up her sweat. I smelled as much like horse as Molly did. We were almost one, Molly and I.

My dad said, gee Molly!

He said, haw Molly!

He said, whoa Molly!

In peach season we hitched Molly between the shafts of a trailer. She stood waiting in the orchard while we took empty baskets from the trailer. Drowsy, one back leg bunched, you've seen how horses stand at rest. We filled the baskets with peaches. We set them back on the trailer. When the trailer was full, my dad drove Molly to the yard for a fresh load of empty baskets. Some days Molly slept between trailer loads. Other days she got hungry. If she saw a full basket of peaches on the ground nearby, she took the trailer along and went off to eat peaches.

Whoa, Molly!

Back, Molly!

I wasn't old enough to pick peaches, but old enough to carry baskets to and from the trailer. And old enough to feed Moly a damaged peach. Molly loved peaches, but sometimes she smashed the trailer into a peach tree. We had to put a nose bag on her. We had to fix the trailer.

Molly. Trotting through my waking hours and days. Galloping through my dreams. In spring, the way she pranced and carried her head. Her feathered mane. Her flowing tail. There was nothing abstract about Molly, nothing you could confuse like you could the commandments. Molly was the most physical thing I knew. I felt a great kindness for Molly, and I wonder if she realized.

I asked my new girlfriend about the psychology of the horse; she's big on psychology anyway. What do you know about the psychology of the horse, I said. And she spun to look at me. She raised her eyebrows high, and then she giggled. That left me confused. I haven't been able to figure out why she was laughing. What was it about my horse question? Or was it because in that moment I'd called her girlfriend rather than partner? If you're my girlfriend, I said, maybe you can tell me. Girlfriend, partner, mate. The truth is, in this 21st century, I don't know what to call her, how to name our relationship. Man and woman, I guess.

Robert Kroetsch again, *Seed Catalogue:*

How do you grow a poet?
. . . .

        This is a prairie road.
        This road is the shortest distance
        Between nowhere and nowhere.
        This road is a poem.

The lecture of danger and daring, *Daniel.*

The first book I touched with my hand was almost certainly a Bible. The same German family Bible. It lay on a low shelf in the corner of the dining room where I would have groped with my fingers for support in my progress from crawling, to standing, to toddling. The shelf, to the Bible, to the chair, and then a few unsteady steps into the room, perhaps landing on my bum, perhaps in my sister's arms. The first book I heard read aloud was a Bible. I heard it read in church, and at home. In German, and not in English until perhaps when I was ten or twelve years old.

We were a family of readers. My father read a variety of newspapers both in German and in English—*The St. Catharines Standard, Der Bote, Die Mennonitische Rundschau.* Evenings and Sundays, or if it was stormy, days he couldn't work. Rain was good for the orchard, and it granted a couple of hours off. He sat in the large, cushioned chair in the living room and read. Sometimes, tired from his work outside, his reading glasses slipped from his nose, and he fell asleep.

My mother read letters, often when she couldn't sleep. At the dining room table, with a writing pad under her right hand, in the process of writing back. Letters from her brother, the only sibling to have survived through birth and childhood. Letters from her nieces. Letters from uncles and aunts, from our adopted Grossmama. From friends. All in German. Most of them from Manitoba. Manitoba, where all us kids were born, the place I thought of as the promised land, I couldn't understand why we'd left.

My sisters read too, in their bedrooms. Lying in bed with their heads propped on one elbow. Story after story, book after book. Books passing from sister, to sister, to sister. My one brother didn't read, or I never saw him, but he did later have a stack of *Time* magazines in his basement bedroom. I remember one or two children's books in our home that might have been given to us as Christmas presents by Sunday school teachers. The loaves and fishes book with a tall bearded Jesus on the cover. But mostly I don't remember children's books at all. The books I grew up with were all for advanced readers. I was the youngest, and I felt crazy sometimes finding everyone's nose pressed to a collection of papers.

And I was crazy to learn how to read. Even before I started off to school. Once I memorized the letters I could sound the words off the page. After that I only needed practice. And I practiced. Sometimes my sisters helped me. I learned to skip the words I didn't know; I became a reader. After a while even the more difficult words began to make sense. I didn't know about the dictionary yet, or how to use it, and I don't imagine we had one in the house.

I read the Hardy Boys. I read Nancy Drew. I read Rin Tin Tin. Even Danny Orlis. I read The Bobbsey Twins. My elementary school kept two or three shelves of books at the front of each classroom, and I read them. In Grade 2, I read the Grade 4 books; in Grade 4, I read the Grade 6 books. *My Friend Flicka. Call of the Wild. Black Beauty.* Any book with a dog or horse in it was sure to catch my attention. Any book set in the wild. My teachers sent me to the principal's office to borrow her books. She kept a few bookshelves of her own. *White Fang. Treasure Island. Kidnapped. The Adventures of Huckleberry Finn. The Last of the Mohicans.*

I read at night before I went to bed. And I read under the bedcovers with a flashlight after curfew. I read at school when I tired of the teacher, a book open on my lap, nothing at all to do with my listening skills. I got in trouble for that, breaking some commandment or other. *Thou shalt listen to the teacher.* I tried to read at the supper table, but my father threatened to strap me. Sometimes I snuck a book into church and read there. A risky thing to do. I wish I could remember a tenth of the books I read before I finished high school.

I read. I devoured books. And each book I opened seemed to take me one step farther from the family Bible. Reading can be dangerous. Reading is a subversive act, and should be.

━━━━━━━

And now *Esther*, a lecture about heroes.

That old family Bible poked its covers from the dusty shelves at the back of my mind a few months ago and I felt as though I'd been struck by lightning. When I left home in my late teens to attend university in Manitoba, I left everything behind. I left my family behind. I left my Mennonite culture behind; I thought I did. And I certainly left the Bible behind. I felt that, although Mennonites still named the Bible as their authority, they had fallen from their original understanding, that they'd betrayed the Bible, that they'd given up their important counter-cultural ways. The Bible in a curious way came to stand as a symbol for what I'd left behind. And choosing a Bible for that class in diversity—my city life felt as distant from the Bible of my childhood as it did from the village grain elevator.

When I arrived in Manitoba I met Margaret Laurence. She was writer-in-residence at the University of Toronto that year and I didn't meet her in person, but I met her books and that was enough. I don't know how it happened. Those books seemed to fall like manna from heaven. They appeared under Christmas trees; they fell from birthday boxes. Friends passed them on to friends. They seemed to show up everywhere. Ask any Canadian reader what their first Canadian reading experience was. Ask any Canadian reader of the 1970s who their favourite Canadian author was. I imagine most of them would hold up Margaret Laurence books. Everyone read Margaret Laurence. There's one Canada before Laurence, and there's another Canada after Laurence. The time after Laurence's earliest publications brought an explosion of Canadian writing. When I read Margaret Laurence, I felt as though I'd suddenly come awake.

I had several Canadian writing mothers and Laurence was the first of them. As I imagine she was a mother for many. We cut our teeth on the pages of her writing. Like Rachel in *A Jest of God*, we came of age and found a fragile selfhood. Like Stacey in *The Fire-Dwellers*, we were trapped, imprisoned, we burned and battled to escape. Like Vanessa in *A Bird in the House*, we explored the cruelty and the sorrow of our childhoods. With Hagar, *The Stone Angel*, we fought and bled for love. *The river runs both ways*—Laurence's truth in parable and paradox, in images and stories. Those stories, we discovered, told the stories of our lives. Stories full of broken commandments, they told the story of my life.

With Morag in *The Diviners*, and with Laurence herself, we Canadian readers abandoned marriages and more practical lives to become writers. Margaret Laurence told the Canadian story. And Margaret Laurence gave us a voice, as did Alice Munro. In 1981 words came to me in my sleep. Out of chaos, out of the dark night. In 1981, I began to write.

Robert Kroetsch:

How do you grow a prairie town?

> The gopher was the model.
> Stand up straight:
> telephone poles
> grain elevators
> church steeples.
> Vanish suddenly: the
> gopher was the model.

The theatre of grief, a lecture of *Lamentations*.

What is it that separates one particular family member from the others? That causes one sibling to leave all that he knows, to run off and live two thousand kilometres from the rest of the family? Is that strictly a coming of age? To leave his culture and place of origin behind, while his siblings remain comfortably settled in the home church and community. What is it pulls or pushes him away? He, she, they. Turns one sibling into a poet and wanderer, while the rest of the family remain teachers, accountants, nurses, housewives, administrators. They choosing from the standard palette of life alternatives, and this one always choosing to be contrary.

If you've travelled by car in sheep country, Syria, Iceland, South Africa, if you've travelled in sheep country, you've no doubt noticed. A flock of a hundred or two hundred white and woolly sheep scattered across the landscape. With white and woolly gambolling lambs. And there, lost but conspicuous, at the edge of the flock, looking always that small amount leaner and more traveled, one shrill black sheep, looking always more recklessly shorn.

When I was a boy, I told my mother that I thought even Hindus, if they were good Hindus, should be allowed into heaven. Not that I thought of her in any way as the gatekeeper. I suppose I meant if they, the Hindus, obeyed the bulk of the commandments. Most of the commandments most of the time. I thought she might be pleased with my generosity. She wasn't. Our church in Southern Ontario sent missionaries to India to evangelize the Hindus, to save them and turn them from their pagan ways. To give them proper clothes, or clothes at all, and make them Christian. Hindus in heaven? It was a terrible heresy, in a childhood where even Catholics or Lutherans wouldn't be granted that privilege. I don't know how I came up with such a notion, maybe I'd misread my Sunday school lessons. Or maybe I was trying already to negotiate a path for *myself*.

In the case of sheep, of course, we know the black comes from a recessive gene. But the human black sheep, the family black sheep, what causes that? Where does the human black sheep element come from? Is it also a matter of genetics, is it caused by string fragments hidden in the DNA? The nature versus nurture debate, what shapes our individual personality traits and behaviour? Is there one moment in childhood when the course of the black-sheep child's life changes? The sins of the parents upon the children unto the third and fourth generation.

Psychologists might define the black sheep as the member of a tightly triangulated family, a dysfunctional family, who holds the rest together in their identification of him as the problem or deviant. As the one who causes all the family difficulties, who brings the family members embarrassment and shame. And the family unites around the task of trying to keep the black sheep in line, to keep him from revealing family secrets. In that sense he's a blessing for them; if they didn't have him to worry about, they'd have to face their own issues. The black sheep shows up everywhere, in business, in schools, in families, in sports, and always their role is the same; they're the scapegoat that holds groups together. And there are benefits for black sheep. They have the freedom to do whatever they want, to be whoever they want to be. They're always the centre of attention to their team or their family, without the black sheep all groups are threatened.

In praise of black sheep! The pariah status of the black sheep, according to an article in *The Globe and Mail*, is undergoing an image makeover. Hordes of amateur genealogists today surf websites like ancestry.com to dig up notorious relatives. Black sheep, says Tyler Schulze, the originator of Blacksheepancestors.com, black sheep make the family tree more appealing, more interesting.

I begged my father for a horse, but he wouldn't buy me one. If we're going to keep a horse, he said, we need a pasture. He meant that our farm wasn't big enough for horses.

I told him that our old horse, our horse from before the tractor, our horse Molly didn't have a pasture. Remember, I said. Before you sent her for glue. My dad must have forgotten and he needed to think of a new excuse.

Or, I said, we could pull out a few of those peach trees. We could plant a pasture; I hated peach trees anyway. Though I knew already that we sure weren't going to take out a peach orchard so I could keep a horse.

Who's going to take care of it, my father said. And who's going to pay for it. The horse. And the feed.

I will, I said. I'll take care of it. I'll get a job.

Thou art brown but comely, a lecture from the *Song of Solomon*.

A family couple of miles from my house kept a bigger red pony, a sorrel, and they said I could borrow him. The parents said the kids didn't like riding anyway. I bicycled three miles to their house on Saturday. I saddled and bridled Red. I stretched out the stirrups. I led him out of the barn and got on his back. The parents had warned me. As soon as I got on his back, Red tried to lie down and roll over. That was his trick, but it didn't work with me. I poked him with my heels and pulled up the reins. And then Red and I went for a ride. We went riding with Paul and Lady. Sometimes we took beans and wieners and we stopped near the railroad track for a fire and cookout.

Every Saturday that Red tried his trick on me, he never quit trying. Stubborn old Red. But it didn't work, even once. I rode him till my legs almost dragged on the ground. I was embarrassed to be riding a pony when my legs were so long, and I told my uncles he was a Welsh pony. I said, Welsh ponies are bigger than Shetlands. They said, maybe he's Welsh, and maybe your legs are far too short for a real horse. I was a tall kid anyway, long and gangly, and they teased me because I looked like a giant on Red's back. I didn't like being teased but I didn't hate it enough to stop riding.

I started back up on my dad again. I told him I needed my own horse to ride. I needed a tall horse.

I recounted this story for my new partner, and she thought about it for a while. In integral thinking, she said finally, the horse is a poem. Is that what you wanted me to say, she said.

I think she and I are beginning to understand each other.

Sometime in 1981 or 82, I wrote my first poem. It wasn't so much that I decided to become a writer, or even to write a poem. Though I admit I harboured a secret wish to turn my pen to something that could be read by others—and that long ago I still did write with a pen. But it wasn't a decision, to sit down and write a poem. Finally, to become a writer. I couldn't even imagine the career of writer as a possibility; I can barely imagine it now. It wasn't that I decided anything, it was that poems began to come to me.

You probably all know the Charles Dickens line, "it was the best of times, it was the worst of times." In my case that quote didn't hold true, it was clearly the worst of times for me, a time of incredulity. The early 1980s. A time of confusion and terror, of grief, my partner and I had developed relationship trouble and had separated, my second relational failure. I'll spare you the details. They're nothing you haven't heard a hundred times. But in all that turmoil, I began to wake in the middle of the night with phrases and sentences in my mind, on my tongue. Silly as it sounds, it suggests the notion of the Biblical prophet, of divine inspiration. At least for someone with my upbringing, and I confess I was tempted to that.

And I call this lecture *Isaiah*.

I'd wake in the morning, having forgotten my visions, and feel I'd lost something valuable. This message from beyond. What were the words? What did they mean? I began to keep pencil and notepad beside my bed. When I woke in the dark night I'd scribble a few key words on the paper. I'd sleep and wake again. Scribble again. In my waking free-time I began to organize those scribblings, to pair them, and move them around on the page. I'd hardly even read poetry, and suddenly I had the gall to write it. An age of foolishness. Lots of troubled sleep, lots of scribbling. Soon I had a bunch of poems, love poems most of them.

I packaged two dozen of them and took them to a writer friend of mine, a professor at the University of Manitoba. My current partner, when she reads those old poems—integral thinking or no—insists if I'd written poems like that for her, she would have dumped me too. I took them to my friend at the university and he said he'd be happy to look at them, he asked me to come back in a week.

I did, I came back a week later. Hey, my friend said, taking up his role as professor, it's great you've decided to become a poet, he said, but these are terrible poems. So much for Isaiah and the notion of divine inspiration. My friend professor dictated a long list of poets to read: bpNichol, Michael Ondaatje, and Phyllis Webb. Cummings, Whitman, and Dickinson. Purdy, Zwicky, Atwood, and McKay. The list read on and on.

He said my poems were too abstract, that he needed my language to be more physical. I didn't even know what he meant. He said he didn't want me ever to use the word lonely in a poem again. He said if I wanted to write about loneliness, I should set a man eating his dinner at the kitchen table, and then place an empty chair across the table. That's how you write about loneliness, he said. Or write about a light bulb, he said, hanging in the middle of an empty room. He talked about physicality, about images. And I puzzled about that for the next few years.

Robert Kroetsch writes:

But how do you grow
a poet?

I was drinking with Al Purdy. We went round and round
in the restaurant on top of the Chateau Lacombe. We
were the turning centre in the still world, the winter
of Edmonton was hardly enough to cool our out-sights.

The waitress asked us to leave. She was rather insistent;
we were bad for business, shouting poems at the paying
customers.

What does it all mean? A text of *Ecclesiastes*.

If you look at the writing of Eduardo Galeano in *Memory of Fire*, or
Kristjana Gunnars in *The Prowler*, of Dany Laferrière in *An Aroma of Coffee*,
you see a prose that tells its story in fragments. In short chapters of a page,
or a half-page, even a quarter-page in length. Hundreds of short chapter
fragments, hundreds of prose poems. A book-length collection of prose
poems, or a long prose poem.

You notice the leap from one story fragment to another, one thought
to the next, and wonder about connecting syntax. You wonder about the
absence of explanation, of the lettered bridge of bones that would trace the
growth of a story from the first fragment to the second. From the second
to the third, third to the fourth, to the fifth. You wonder about the missing
link. You notice the reticence of plot and storyline, as if plot and storyline
haven't yet been discovered. As if the story, after a paragraph or two, loses
its way. As if it needs to take its first steps over and over. To always begin
again. As if the writer were more concerned with beginnings than with
connections and conclusions, than with meaning.

My partner asks about this. Remember her concern for inter-relatedness,
for the connection between things. We're traveling the world of food, she

and I, and today we're eating Ethiopian. Lamb and lentils, injera, wat and tibs. No forks and knives, no utensils at all. Fun to eat this way, with your fingers, the memories of a childhood. Licking your fingers. Why, she says, lifting a handful of injera and chicken, why do your favourite writers, your favourite poets, write this way? Why this scattered kind of writing. Why don't they tell the whole story?

Maybe, I answer, they've had too many difficult days at the computer or notepad, and grown lazy, Gunnars and Galeano, Laferrière, too lazy to write the fillers their story fragments require, to engrave connecting paragraphs. Ha! Their eyes hurt, their wrists and elbows, I'm teasing. But then seriously, maybe they're too much the poet, envisioning each paragraph of prose as already fulfilled, completed, needing no explanation. Or maybe they feel their scattered writing best reflects the nature of our lives, our memories, fragmentary and inconclusive. Or that the notion of neatly intertwined warp and weft, of complete and chronicled tapestry, is too fixed for the range of their experience.

Maybe the conventional connecting paragraph draws conclusions and interpretations that are too easy, too decisive, where the absence of connector allows more subtlety and a greater complexity of meaning, even of paradox. Gunnars and Galeano, Laferrière, I suggest to her, they question the very idea of genre, creating a text that defies convention and definition. They place both themselves and the reader in the gap between stories. The body of the reader drawn into the space between story fragments, an invitation to discomfort, an invitation to discovery, to question, to imagination. Challenging the reader to piece together the components of a story, to make their own sense of it. Gunnars and Galeano, they enjoy the honesty of revealing the holes in their stories, in their lives. And since everything's interrelated anyway, they feel they don't need to bother with the obvious. What do you think, I say, do you think that's a possible reading? That Galeano and Gunnars resist the literalists and the concrete reading of their scriptures. And isn't the Bible itself a fragmented text?

Psalms and Proverbs, you can lead a horse to water.

The horse was named Lady, but she wasn't much of one. Not much of a lady, nothing prim and proper for her. She was a crazy horse for sure. She never stopped dancing and prancing, frothing at the mouth. She wanted to run; Lady lived to run. It was her battle against oppression.

Paul told me I could take her for a ride, and I slow galloped her down an old gravel road a couple miles from home. Nice day for a ride. The spring sun above. The breeze against my face and chest. The squeal of the saddle. My boot in the stirrup. And me, on a full-sized horse. I wished my school friends could see me. I wished my uncles could see me.

I say a slow gallop down the gravel road, that was for the first minute. Then it became a demented and dancing spiral down the road. Foam slashing from her mouth. Feet lifted high and neck arched. This crazy horse. The reins in my hand stretched tight as guitar strings. She wouldn't tire, and she wouldn't settle down. I thought I'd give her just a taste of what she wanted. I gave her a bit more rein.

Have you ever ridden a quarter horse? The fastest creature in the quarter mile. From dancing circle to full speed in about two and a half seconds. Damn! That was Lady! After a hundred yards, and two hundred, she only seemed to run harder. Run faster. And faster still. I pulled on the reins and leaned back to try and stop her. She wouldn't stop. Lady ran. I levered back and forth on her bridle. She ran. The road we ran on had deep ditches either side or I would have turned and raced her in a big circle round a field. I thought of that, but Lady thought only of running.

I got scared. There was a paved road crossing about a half mile ahead, I could see the cars. Reins, I knew, could be torn, and bridles broken, I didn't dare pull back any harder. Or longer. I decided to see if I could wear her out—I leaned forward and dug my heels into her ribs, I kicked her ribs. I don't know if you've ever been on a runaway horse, it's a sensation like no other.

I did finally manage to get Lady stopped. More accurately, Lady managed finally to wear herself out. Lucky the road was long enough. And when I got off her back my knees shook so I could hardly stand. That Lady horse didn't bow to holy scripture, mine, or my dad's, or anybody's. She was her own scripture. I wasn't her lord at all, though she wasn't exactly mine either. The smell of her. I loved that horse, and she terrified me. I've never been that frightened in my life, yet here we stood side by side.

Physical poems. Poems you can touch and taste. Robert Kroetsch again:

How do you grow a poet?
. . . .

> Son, this is a crowbar.
> This is a willow fencepost.
> This is a sledge.
> This is a roll of barbed wire.
> This is a bag of staples.
> This is a claw hammer.

The calm and comfort of *Job*.

I have an apple story to tell you. I can guess what you're thinking, and you're wrong. The story has nothing to do with nakedness, almost nothing. And there's no snake in the story. Unless you read the physical manifestation of the strap as a snake, but that would turn the story upside down.

It wasn't at all difficult to get the strap at my house. I don't know about my brother and sisters, my friends, and I don't know about you in your childhood, but I got the strap often enough. My father kept a piece of gray buffalo leather in the basement. An inch wide, twenty-four inches long, a quarter inch thick. My sisters and I agreed it was buffalo because of the way it stung, buffalo must surely sting more than cow. Sometimes father used that, the leather, sometimes he used his bare hand. Hand or leather, neither gave us much satisfaction.

The apple? One of those green apples, the Granny Smith kind. The soil on our seven-acre farm in Niagara wasn't much good for growing apples, but we traded each year. Traded canning peaches for a bushel of apples. With a farmer living only a few miles down the road but closer to the escarpment where apples flourished—the escarpment home of the Niagara

Falls. And we kept those apples in our basement where it was cooler, where they wouldn't spoil.

My father found a Granny Smith apple in the orchard with three small bites taken out of it. Child-sized bites, not grown-up bites. And he took us all, his children, into the basement and lined us up, oldest to youngest, against the wall. Not all his children, the oldest two were already married or away from home. Our basement always smelled damp and mouldy. It was dark, only one light bulb, and the ceiling hung low. Yes, we were backed up against the wall.

Father held the apple in his hand to show and asked my brother, the oldest present. Did you take a bite out of this apple and throw it in the orchard?

Brother said, I didn't, no. He sounded confident.

He asked the sister who was next. Did you take a bite out of the apple and throw it in the orchard?

Sister was never timid about anything. She said, no.

He asked the next three sisters and they all said no.

I was last. My father asked me. Did you take a bite out of an apple and throw it in the orchard?

The temptation was great. Or maybe I really hadn't done it—I don't like Granny Smith apples to this day. Did I throw the apple in the orchard after tasting it? Was it bitter, was it too green? The temptation was great. No, I said. I thought it might work, it worked for the others, but maybe my hands were shaking. And what chance did I have anyway.

And sure, I was the one who got the strap. One for wasting an apple and two for lying. It was probably a test, like for Adam and Eve in the garden, or Job, and I failed it. I can't remember which commandment I broke. It wasn't about idols or swearing, and I was too young to dance. And I hadn't stolen anything.

Some years later, on a Sunday, I got the strap because I refused to pray. We had company, a giant preacher in a black suit and thunder in his voice visiting after church, all of us sitting round the table ready to eat. No apples on the table anywhere, not even apple sauce. My father asked me to pray before the meal, it was our custom for someone to pray. And it would have been easy, just to repeat the simple verse we always used, but I shook my head. No, I wasn't going to pray. No.

I must have been angry with him; he must have said something, done something, to make me mad. Maybe I felt shy or afraid because of the visitor, but probably not. My father asked again. I turned, lowered my eyes, and stared at my plate. It was a startling moment of rebellion, and I don't know how I dared. Not only to disobey, but stubborn intention, and in front of witnesses, in front of this particular witness. My father took me into the basement where I lowered my pants, here the almost nakedness, and bent over so he could thrash me. *Obey thy father and thy mother*, I knew the commandment I'd broken.

We weren't always adversaries my father and I, but on that day, I understood fully that he wanted to rule not only my hands and feet, what I did, but even my mouth, the sounds I made, and my thoughts. He seemed always to have his big blacksmith hand on the back of my neck, for steering and control. And here, this son always choosing to be contrary. It was the one time that buffalo leather brought me satisfaction, there'd been a battle and I knew that I'd won.

But I need to confess that I've been lying to you. That business of the girlfriend, the new woman partner who keeps showing up in these notes, I confess that she's pure fiction. I invented her for the sake of the story, I'm as single today as the day I left home as a teenager. And the business with the pop-bottle two and ten cents, I'm not sure that's accurate. It might have been one and five. Same with the dimensions of the gray leather strap. The runaway horse was true enough, though I can't remember whether I really did lean forward and give her the heels to make her run faster. But it's a good story that way. And the twenty-four lectures for this evening. Another fabrication. Telling lies. Like breaking commandments, you see how easy it is. If you start young, and once it catches in your blood. And that's how I became a writer. Fiction, as one Abraham Verghese character states, is the lie that tells the truth about how the world lives.

⁂

And a lecture called *Revelations*. A curious thing happened when my father died.

In North American culture, the stereotype suggests, when parents die, all the grown children get together to quarrel about furniture, and dishes, and cutlery. About family heirlooms. About money. About property. To argue about who gets what. It doesn't seem to matter what the will says. In some cases, what the will says only makes the bickering worse.

In my family, among my siblings, I'm sure this post-funeral process of dividing the remains of my mother and father's life together was a relatively simple one. My mother, I should tell you here, had died some twenty years earlier, and my father had been downsizing ever since. The post-funeral dividing of remains was a simple one, I'm sure. I say, I'm sure. But I don't know because, being the black sheep of the family, I wasn't there. When my father died at 92, he still lived on his own in a small apartment in Niagara. And he left only a few small rooms of belongings, my father wasn't a collector. There wasn't much to argue about. And nothing of great value. Hardly a couch, or a dresser, or table that anybody wanted.

There *were* hundred-pound bags of flour and rice in the back storage. My father, while in his teens, experienced the famine in Ukraine following the Bolshevik Revolution, and he *always* thought about backup. But this rice by now was infested with bugs, as was the flour, and nobody wanted either of them. I wasn't there, and neither was my dad, to remind the siblings that, should famine come, they'd be happy to eat rice, bugs and all. And there were several four-litre containers of kerosene, but no one owned a kerosene lamp anymore or remembered how to operate one.

And when the rest of my father's possessions had been divided, after a few hours trading as I imagine it, they came to the two family Bibles. Large books, both of them, heavy books, I mean in pounds, one English and scarcely used, the other German and badly in need of repair. I assume, sitting here at my desk in Winnipeg, suddenly realizing that with everything divided they'd forgotten to leave anything for the prodigal, my siblings decided to send the Bibles to me.

Imagine my surprise! And they all churchgoers and practising Christians. They didn't want the Bibles, those symbols of their faith and their origins. And I hear your mental gears churning. I hear them working, grinding. You think it was a kind of manipulation, a hope that they would somehow, by sending me the Bibles, turn me from my ungodly ways. I choose not to think so. I think they recognized that in my appreciation for books, for word, for text, for story, in my vocation as writer, I would have more use for the family Bibles than any of them.

And now these two Bibles have come to rest on my bookshelves in Winnipeg. And some days I take them from my library and lay them on a table to look up a story. I lay them on the table because they need space and support. When some biblical character appears in my dreams, in my wandering. Demands to enter a story or poem I'm working on. The story of Jacob wrestling with the angel. The story of Noah and the flood. The story of Ruth, of Judas. I look up the narrative. I compare the nuance of language or translation; I have other smaller Bibles. I wonder at the stories' imagery.

I'm always looking up favourite stories. Stories written by Alice Munro. Or Cormac McCarthy. By Isabel Allende and Carol Shields. I look for technical solutions to my own writing problems. I look for physical images, things you can see or hold. I look for hope. Is this a story of redemption, or a story of despair.

These Bibles still resting on my bookshelves. Symbols of my culture of origin and, I suppose, symbols of my current culture. No longer the sacred texts they once were, but symbols for all that's sacred in text and story, symbols for the holiness of life. There they lie, two Bibles on my bookshelves, with all my other books.

⁓⁓⁓⁓⁓⁓

And finally, the lecture called *Judith*.

Why do we tell stories? Why do people tell so many stories? Why do we gather round the fire? Or the kitchen table, or the bar, to talk? Why do children find joy, or comfort, or sorrow, in their parents' histories? Tell me about when you were little. Tell me about Grandma. Why does the room go quiet, and everyone lean forward to catch the words?

My grandfather, when he reached the age of ten in Scotland, chased all his older brothers over the ravine. It was a matter of convention and inheritance. Let me explain.

The sky turned black, and the wind howled. All the farmer's chickens came to roost in the middle of the afternoon. It was a Sunday and Juni happened to be tucked in her favourite chair by the fireplace.

My great aunt, Matilda, as a girl in Australia thought she was a kangaroo. Wanted to be a kangaroo. She sewed herself a pouch for her belly and started off to hatch a tail. Not an easy project even at her age. "And the band played Waltzing Matilda."

Stories imagined, or remembered, if there's any difference. The world bursts with stories, with story seeds, and people telling. The world lives by story, breathes it, bristles with it. The television, the radio, the library. The telephone, computer. Wires and wind whispering with story. Tree leaves telling a tale.

Sometimes it's the wine. Or the moon. The time of day. Sometimes it's love, we call it love. A friend we haven't seen for thirteen years. Someone asks a question; someone asks whether you like horses.

Horses! The question bumps you to the back of your chair. And you begin. Molly, you say, had a brown coat, and a black mane and tail, and long white hair around her hooves. The story. It's a moment of love, of joy, anger.

Sometimes I wish I could just be healed. Today would be good. Sometimes the anguish feels like lead, almost more than I can carry. Why do I tell the story? What would happen if I stopped?

I'm playing with a pail and shovel under the giant willow tree while the cicadas sing in the branches above. A hot day, sunny, and I pull a story from deep in the squared sandbox. I wipe it clean, try to, with my hand. Hold it under the spout of the hand pump for water. Wipe again. But the dirt won't wash away.

I wake one morning in a tent in Taman Negara, in the heart of Malaysia, and discover a chronicle standing by the side of the bed. A fabled shape, dark and amorphous, with tentacles. Before I can jump up to chase it away, it speaks to me. Here's the story the chronicle tells.

Dickens, Charles. *A Tale of Two Cities*. London: Chapman & Hall, 1859.

Kroetsch, Robert. *Seed Catalogue. Completed Field Notes: The Long Poems of Robert Kroetsch*. University of Alberta Press, 2000.

Verghese, Abraham. *The Covenant of Water*. Grove Press, 2023.

White, Patrick. "Black sheep, good sheep." *The Globe and Mail*, 19 June 2007, https://www.theglobeandmail.com/life/black-sheep-good-sheep/article20404685/

ACKNOWLEDGEMENTS AND NOTES

Poems from *Where Calling Birds Gather* (2013) are reprinted here with the kind permission of Turnstone Press. Lines from Robert's Kroetsch's long poem *Seed Catalogue* (in *Completed Field Notes*, 2000) are quoted with the kind permission of University of Alberta Press.

Thanks to Manitoba Arts Council, Winnipeg Arts Council, and Canada Council for the Arts for assistance over the course of my career; to publishers Turnstone Press, Broken Jaw Press, Wolsak and Wynn, and Punchpenny Press for their support of my work; and to Winnipeg Public Library and University of Winnipeg residency programs for giving me time to write.

Thanks for their careful reading go to George Amabile (*After the Revolution*), David Arnason (*Ride the Blue Roan*), Krista Rothmaler (*Violinmaker's Lament*), Douglas Reimer, Sean Virgo, and Susan Stratford (*Coils of the Yamuna*), Wayne Tefs (*Under the Wings of Africa*), Victor Enns and Dennis Cooley (*Where Calling Birds Gather*).

Many of these poems first appeared in *Anerca, Arts Manitoba, Center for Mennonite Writing Journal, edges, Hub City, Mennonite Mirror, Prairie Fire, Prairie Journal of Canadian Literature, Rhubarb, Rainbow Papers*, and *A/Cross Sections: New Manitoba Writing*.

Some poems have been lightly revised for this edition; in *Coils of the Yamuna* some of the poems have been retitled.

The chapbook *Twelve Poems for Emily Carr* was inspired by her writing in *Hundreds and Thousands: The Journals of Emily Carr* (Douglas & McIntyre, 2006; first published in 1966).

Finally, we've decided it might be helpful to reproduce this short section of the Introduction to *Under the Wings of Africa*:

But you wanted a story. A story of travel. A story of South Africa. A story of love and of sorrow. How much of this story is true? you ask. You're asking me? Yes, I'll leave aside all deception. The story is true. It's all true, for me; every word of this chronicle true. Even the lies are true.

INDEX OF POEMS